Torn Wings and Faux Pas

Torn Wings
and Faux Pas

A Flashbook of Style,
A Beastly Guide
Through the Writer's Labyrinth

Karen Elizabeth Gordon

Illustrations by Rikki Ducornet

Pantheon Books
New York

All rights reserved under International and Pan-American
Copyright Conventions. Published in the United States by
Pantheon Books, a division of Random House, Inc., New York,
and simultaneously in Canada by Random House
of Canada Limited, Toronto.

Library of Congress Cataloging-in-Publication Data

Gordon, Karen Elizabeth.
Torn wings and faux pas : a flashbook of style, a beastly guide
through the writer's labyrinth / Karen Elizabeth Gordon.
p.   cm.
Includes index.
ISBN 0-679-44242-1
1. English language—Grammar.   2. English language—
Usage.   I. Title.
PE1112.G579   1997
428.2—dc21   97-11232

Random House Web Address: http://www.randomhouse.com

Book design by M. Kristen Bearse

Printed in the United States of America
First Edition
2   4   6   8   9   7   5   3   1

for
Jann Donnenwirth

Acknowledgments

THANKS IN MANY WAYS to Camilla Collins, Paul Walker, Maureen Jung, Maia Gregory, Rikki Ducornet, Steven Moore, Holly Johnson, Milo Radulovich, Jann Donnenwirth, Alba Witkin, Jean-Jacques Passera, Danielle Mémoire, Denny Leuer, Irene Bogdanoff Romo, Drago Rastislav Mrazovac, and my editor, Shelley Wanger.

Introduction

IT IS MANY YEARS NOW since I began concocting linguistic ambrosias wrapped around insufferable tidings. Just as I think I've abandoned the genre, it clamors once again for a send-up, bellowing out my name. Since I am much more drawn to vocabulary, imagination, fluency, and fluidity than strictures of structure, grammatical chastity belts, and rules, I tilted this book (at a rakish angle) into the territory of usage, which is also rife with potential faux pas—false steps—and terrors. *Torn Wings and Faux Pas* is a focused, fast, revolving alphabet of style and usage, an emergency roadside and night flight rescue for writers with their myriad perplexities. Creatures from imaginary landscapes lead you, puzzled or curious, by the paw through an alphabet of uncertainties, where the most rampant errors and fears are explored: word nuances and abuses, spelling confusions, and preferable usage. Other issues this flashbook illuminates, explodes, deplores, and exonerates are double negatives, split infinitives, painful separations (misplacements of various sorts), parallel construction, consistency in voice, tense, mood, and person, and dangling modifiers. The grand finale of all this drama is a section on sentence creation and combination, winding up at the Schloss where so many rowdy weekends are taking place—with its cast of butler, panther, au pair, general factotum, absent owner (Drasko

Mustafović, off with his band of brigands), baby dragons with their nanny, and orgiastic guests.

The book itself is an orgy, in fact—an orgy of orthography, shifting positions, inter-species fraternizing, naughtiness given safe conduct by stylistic panache and grammatical gravitas. Sultry sirens lure you through depths of understanding, below the surfaces skimmed in *The Deluxe Transitive Vampire*. On the tail of a big bad panther or the trail of a lipsmacking dragon, you will skulk about the naughty Schloss of earthly and unearthly pleasures and find among them the thrill of writing adventurously, with raffish precision and lucid *volupté*. Rivers of stories running through Azuriko carry us on to other strangely familiar lands: Lavukistan, Blegue, and the mournful Trajikistan.

Torn Wings and Faux Pas completes *The Deluxe Transitive Vampire*. A handful of characters from that book appear among a flurry of new figures, with their madcap and macabre mischief: Angie Canasta, Dante Kaputo, Ziggie Spurthrast and a sabotaged sous-chef aboard the *Scarlatina,* a sorceress, turbaned serpents, banditti, and mercenaries at war, a dynasty of kings—the Incognito succession—and a defenestrated (and feathered) duchess. Various felines are on the prowl, one with an injured paw pausing mid-air beside many a verbal faux pas.

I have also conjured, then called upon, a collection of language luminaries, whom I claim to have met as a surprise guest on Startling Glower's "Up Your Eponym" television program. The surprise was on me: they and the camera crew invaded my villa in Louvelandia and forced me to participate. I retaliated by kidnapping them into this book, exposing their backgrounds to clarify their distinctive demeanors and perspectives.

You might well wonder why I devote any space to the childhoods of these eccentric, contentious authorities. Childhood is where we acquire such dazzling sophistication, our sentence structures and lexicons developing right along with our physiognomies and bones, complexes and phobias, aberrations and dreams. In the middle of "aberration" comes the word "err," which in our writing we seek to avoid. But erring is also wandering, without which we would discover nothing of the world or of ourselves. If we tear our wings, gash our souls in the process, we will remember how we happened upon such knowledge, and what it means to us. That is why the occasional trek to Trajikistan is taken here: some of those travelers return in love.

Authorities Consulted,
Quoted, Exalted, and Exposed

NATTY AMPERSAND WAS ASPHYXIATED on a subjunctive clause at the tender age of eighteen months, which her parents blamed on her English nanny, whom they banished from their New English domicile, along with their darling's nappies and stuffed rats. Rushed to Emergency, Natty was revived by a choral prelude in passive voice, which went over very soothingly and changed her sex in the process—henceforward, she would be a boy. He studied Latin, Greek, Hungarian, and Urdu while other high schoolers were shooting up, and took a flying leap into Cambridge at the age of seventeen, changing sexes there once again (thinking it might be more fun), which he/she has continued to do, alternating as new books emerge. It is as if, she once said in an interview as a woman, the one impregnated the other, ensuring a squalling succession of grammatical brats. I consult Natty when I'm feeling blue: his/her approach is at once antiquated and fresh, classical and revolting, and the rats that disappeared from her childhood bring on a plague of mirth, resurfacing with black bodies, pink toes, and torrid tales from the lower depths—on scraps of paper skewered over their terrible sharp white teeth.

STARTLING GLOWER WAS GLUM as an embryo and suckled his mother's breast with such deadly seriousness that I felt compelled to convey this fact through an awkward prepositional phrase. As his mama was a mournful madonna with a salty mother tongue, Startling could rip to shreds his playmates' toys with a carefully aimed interjection of compounded negatives and unparallel structures (he was an absolute *mishap* at parallel play), shifting tenses and hard, bright words. He shone his own way through prep school and provincial colleges, keeping his mind on the Augustan Age, Pope and his pip-squeaks, the bons mots of Dr. Johnson, till he hit the Restoration stage. There Startling found his true calling, becoming an actor, fop, and playwright of fraudulent Restoration dramas, setting his witticisms to glimmer in the dark. From the stage he leapt—or fell—into the medium of television with his popular show "Up Your Eponym," whose programs will gratify our voyeuristic yearnings every now and then. I have stolen his syntax and sense of timing, and paraphrased his mock-pompous pronouncements on etiquette in sentences and farce.

DRAT SILTLOW CRAWLED OUT of the primal ooze in the late forties, his parents both heroin addicts, great musicians (cembalo, sax), father a descendant of the Northumbrian clan responsible for a nineteenth-century archaeological hoax, mother a vaudevillain's out-of-wedlock child raised by three maiden aunts on candy and the occasional possum in the Appalachian hills—till she joined *her* mother in St. Louis— which is where this doomed and talented pair met and created their first and only child. Drat skulked through grammar school on neuter pronouns and dangled phrases, picked up from his mother's listless hours and trailing-off bedtime stories—then suddenly shot ahead of his class and rocketed into Harvard once the heroin wore off (from that steady nine-month soak). Although he never evinced the slightest aptitude for music (and indeed, his inability to read musical notes seriously threatened his attempts to grasp punctuation), he did inherit his parents' proclivities for improvisation, which underscores his every utterance on linguistic niceties and naughtiness, the latter being his specialty during his frequent appearances on Startling Glower's "Up Your Eponym."

ZOË PLATGUT IS THE ONLY full-time female I've consulted on this book: I like her sensible walking shoes—no frills approach when I am at my wits' end. Oh, sure, she can be lethally literal-minded and flinty, but I just jab her in the ribs with my pencil (eraser end, to avoid lead poisoning), and that lightens her up sufficiently for me to take her bull by the horns. Platgut turned to English grammar after a trigonometrist, a flamenco instructor, and a sheik of one of the Arab Emirates gave up on her (her father was a purveyor of petrol and liked the hospitality; thus Zoë spent several vacations in one of those palatial hotels, drowning in a large armchair while trying to learn Arabic, whose script seemed to promise the grace that was lacking in her movements and her name). In confronting the demons that Platgut embodies for me (not only the innate clumsiness, a bond, an affinity we share, but all this right and wrong stuff: it makes the hairs stand up on my back, when I'm not prone to fainting fits), I discovered her mystical side: monasteries in Macedonia, liturgies for rhythm and concentration, conjugations of sacred texts (an exercise she prefers to crossword puzzles). I've written Zoë fan letters and questions, and always receive crisp replies from her secretary, Moe True. I have folded these into my treatise here, unacknowledged, yet undisguised.

CRAM FOSSILBLAST HAD a pre-historic early childhood, spent the third grade looking at his class through the window, as the teacher locked him out for monosyllabic rough language and pugnacious demeanor toward the teacher's pet (a castrated tomcat named Albion), then caught up with Western Civilization reluctantly in a seventh-grade morphology class (speaking of morphs, he is a mesomorph with crash-helmet cranium and does he ever have taut muscles—and prose—without even trying; his principles are floppier, which is why he's a favorite of mine). Fossilblast's fascination with sentence structure is even more evident in his novels than in his very slim volumes on style (one volume per ordinance, with variations both exemplary and awry), although I've tried to keep his literary production out of *this* volume by stuffing it back into *The Disheveled Dictionary,* whence it came (to me). His send-up of *The Elements of Style* (boxed set, with monogram) instantly became a more classic classic than the object of its ridicule, and it is this work that has inspired me throughout this other travesty you hold in your curious hands.

VARGAS SCRONX,* a Medievalist and Gothic Romancer, lives in a grotto by an English pub. He lent me his dragons, whom I decided to distress, distract, and rob, till I got carried away with the photographs and Alyosha slipped in for some action and wondered what these beasts were hoarding and hiding and set out to beguile them: in other words, to take care of things for me (I thought she was hopelessly obsessed with gargoyles, but dragons offered a new challenge, and she liked the smoke that they snorted, claiming it had mind-enhancing properties without in the least tripping her up). I also got the debutante to divert him long enough (the grotto was child's play after her tête-à-têtes with the troll) for me to steal his Angels of Saxony, his vocabulary, his incunabula, and his wife.[†]

---

* Also known to readers of his popular fiction as Aelfric Valinthrob; I shall use the names interchangeably depending on which one seems to have the upper hand.
[†] She helped out with the typing and Internetting, and inadvertently became the nanny of a bedroom of baby dragons.

Torn Wings and Faux Pas

adverse / averse

⸙ *Adverse* means unfavorable. *Averse,* meaning reluctant or opposed, and taking the preposition *to,* is a more subjective adjective.

The Bleeding Mirrors of Versailles do have an occasional adverse effect on susceptible, time-traveling individuals, but Natasha, who ran past them instead of going to the *toilettes* she'd excused herself to from the side of her solicitous *maman,* experienced her first moments of ecstasy in those glittering *miroirs sanglants* (and as for the *toilettes,* they thrilled her with their *glaces sanglotantes,* or sobbing looking-glasses).

"I would not be averse to a month in Buenos Aires," said the robot to the dentist as he brushed a bit of rust from his partner's ruffles and applied a drop of oil to his own left knee.

affect / effect

❧ While *affect* usually means to influence, to have an effect upon, to change, it shifts its emphasis auditorially to the first syllable and becomes a noun in psychiatry and psychology. Startling Glower once dragged onto the show "Up Your Eponym" a collection of pop psychologists (mincing to their places and sporting moles and affectations, all powdered and dressed up in Restoration frippery to pander to Glower's sartorial and aesthetic proclivities) who discussed "the affect of an abused sibling, crying into her mother's soup" or "a Lothario who was utterly destitute of affect, but handsomely rich in beaux gestes and looks."

❧ *Effects* in certain apparent contexts can also mean goods or belongings:

We were instructed to appear at the dock before midnight, with but one valise each of personal effects.

❧ As a verb, *effect* means to bring about or to cause:

This statute effected a rousing revival of vanishing without a trace.

all

⯛ When *all* modifies a noun, *of* is unnecessary. When a pronoun is what comes next and is thus embraced, *all of* is how to take it all at once.

All the activities on board required social graces, so the second skipper was much obliged to skip all of them and skulk about the deck alone.

All the mermaids at the bottom of the sea are in the thrall of Ziggie Spurthrast.

"I love all of him: his golden curls, his Adriatic Communist childhood, his labyrinth, and his honorable intentions, however maddeningly forever he finds he must suffer to defer them," said Jonquil of the lasting lover she'd met on a mapmaking trek through Trajikistan.

All of us are off to Amplochacha to inspect the mustache on the statue of Prolix XII.

All the rats recalled the night the pizza chef snuffed it.

All of them claimed to have been visiting an aunt stricken with bubonic plague in Louvelandia at the time, and bore witness to each other's protestations.

all ready / already

☙ *Already* is previously; *all ready* takes care of gangs in preparation.

We're all ready for the reception, and she's still upstairs toying with the pistils of her corsage and the revolver in her garter, and shooting up one more time while she brightens her teeth.

The dossier on Monsieur Joubert Plume is all ready to be delivered to the thugs.

"He's already nipped me on the shoulder, and his fangs haven't yet emerged from his gums!" exclaimed the baby vampire's nanny to her colleague as they watched their charges cavorting about the grotto's urn.

all right

☙ *All right* is the correct form; *alright* is to be forgotten. *All right* is hyphenated only when it's appearing as a compound modifier.

"No, it's not all right with me if my gigolo sees you through your door and checks your boudoir for earthquake faults, your bedroom closet for rats," declared Tanagra's mother, Angie Canasta, on her Trastevere terrazzo as her daughter was spicing up her penultimate "Ciao."

He's an all-right gigolo: very obliging in the kitchen.

all together / altogether

☙ *All together* means as a group. *Altogether* means entirely or in all.

Their teeth still bloody from this unholy repast, the vampires decided all together to comb their mustaches and greet the dawn over a game of poker.

That fuchsia-hued frock on the grandfather clock is altogether too picturesque for this dolorous occasion.

Have you gone altogether berserk, or are you certifiably still O.K.?

Altogether there were seventeen impersonators of Incognito VIII during the so-called Cashmere Crisis that muffled the morganatic monarch and discredited his regime.

"We can't proceed with the orgy till we're all together," said the secretary and sergeant-at-arms in unison, looking about for some stragglers, after they'd read the minutes of the last orgy, and the Mardi Gras videotape had aired its buttocks and its bellows and its groans.

allude / elude

☙ To *allude* to something is to refer to it obliquely or briefly. Thus, in this first sentence, the kneecaps might be indicated with rolled eyeballs or a comment about awkward alignment and garters—or they might be mentioned in passing. To *elude* is to evade, escape, avoid, perhaps with a bit of trickery involved, to become tauntingly out of reach. *Elude* can also apply to understanding.

Please do not allude to his knocking kneecaps in mixed company. He's consulted specialists the world over, and even a custom-made wire-rimmed strapless brassiere has failed to rein them in.

We eluded the banditti by taking five right turns in a frenzy of flying petticoats and plunging into a darkness thick as thieves.

I can hardly say that your name, with its many spluttering consonants, is on the tip of my tongue; I recall an initial *Z,* and the final *sz,* but the rest eludes me.

allusion / illusion

꿍 An *allusion* is an indirect reference, while an *illusion* is an impression or a belief that is false, dreamy, imagined, or un-real, however deliciously it might sustain us.

His allusion to *The Sedentary Tzatzkeleh* was embedded in a tirade against hyperactive women in literature and praise of their more placid sisters lazing on estival riverbanks and Levantine divans.

Do not entertain any illusions about our poor country. Contraband, concupiscence, and clashing cymbals are rife on the waterways of Azuriko, and affairs of state are run from a few flimsy pavilions that are frequently carried off by floods.

almost

 Almost is the adverb meaning nearly. *All most* is taking everyone into account and modifying the next apparition in the sentence, as the *most* modifies *pleased* in the second sentence about the baby vampire's relatives.

"I'm almost knowing how to be writing," said the precocious vampire to his nanny.

"We're all most pleased to hear of his precocity!" pronounced his mother, speaking for her far-flung family, from Boston to the Carpathian Mountains.

NOTE: *If Mama Tutulescu had wanted to indicate that she was not thoroughly delighted with her child's talents, she would have said she was almost pleased.*

⁊ Like other tricky adverbs that include *even, hardly, nearly, only,* and *scarcely, almost* wants to be near the word it modifies.

not:
What pride thumped in his mother's breast! The little rabbit almost won every race in the Grand Tournoi of Trajikistan.

but:
What pride thumped in his mother's breast! The little rabbit won almost every race in the Grand Tournoi of Trajikistan.

not:
A Handful of Mist slipped out of my grasp when I almost lost my entire library by skipping off to the Highlands.

not:
A Handful of Mist slipped out of my grasp when I lost my almost entire library by skipping off to the Highlands.

but:
A Handful of Mist slipped out of my grasp when I lost almost my entire library by skipping off to the Highlands.

always / all ways

❧ *Always* means at all times. *All ways* means in all fashions, by all methods.

Loona had always wanted to be a star, but now that success was snapping her photo wherever she went and throwing her into the arms of groupies who grabbed at her earlobes and made off with her hats, stockings, and fake handcuffs, she longed for the gentle cover of obscurity that had once seemed like a doomed estate.

She tried in all ways to discourage such rabid admiration, confessing her follies and questionable proclivities, her weakness for alcoholic concoctions that would put an extraterrestrial on Mars, for men in leather aprons and sandals, for unspeakable velocities in parked cars, but the more she divulged, the wilder about her the fans became, the more obsequiously they fawned and slobbered over her slippers, the more inaccurately they quoted and aped her.

among / between

❧ *Among* announces three or more participants in most goings-on, while *between* introduces a twosome. Pronouns in all such combinations belong in the objective case.

Between you and me lies a chasm of culture and clichés.

Among us are those who would scoff at the chance to make whoopee with that mesomorph.

Between him and her an understanding has arisen that might dispense with further formalities.

Among the guests at the Schloss that weekend reigned a fever of insatiable intrigues.

Laurinda, naked beneath her Hyperborean furs, stalked the craven Ambel Sondquist between the Firemen's Ball and the lake.

BETWEEN SCORCHING herself on the dragon's come-hitherness and snapping his portrait from every angle but beneath, Alyosha was feeling quite wrung out when he offered her a biscuit and tea.

NOTE: *An exceptional circumstance disrupts the neat distinction above, which is why I've delayed its divulgence till now. When three or more items are taken one pair at a time, that relationship comes across through the insertion of* between, *not* among.

Harsh words are currently flying without restraint between the executive producer and the casting, costume, and scenery brigades. The director has made himself scarce and is shuffling between his two mistresses.

amount / number

❧ *Amount* is used for things in bulk, *number* for the quantity of individual items.

There was a staggering amount of lumber tossed this way and that in the jasmine-enwrapped pergola we had chosen for our bodice-ripping assignation.

We staggered over a fearsome number of rough-hewn planks and fallen women to rescue souls and bear away blue and bloated bodies from the raging river.

another

❧ *Another* conveys the idea of duplication when a quantity has already been stated; it does not mean *additional*.

not:
Eight dope fiends were passed out, another four were merely giddy in the empyrean.

but:
Eight dope fiends were passed out, another eight floated
on high.

or:
Eight dope fiends were passed out, four others flew past the
pearly gates.

anticipate / expect

꙳ *Expectation* is a state of mind; *anticipation* is both a state
of mind and some sort of preparatory action or behavior.
This is true of the verb forms as well.

We'll expect you at the trattoria. I'll be wearing last year's
domino, my wife, her sapphire bustier.

Jonquil, anticipating Torquil's tantrum, arranged to meet him
before the holy relics of Amplochacha's cathedral. He couldn't
very well call her a bitch and slash his wrists in sight of Santa
Archulaga.

anxious / eager

🍂 Zoë Platgut states that one cannot be anxious about anything without dread, insomnia, or anxiety. An eager person might experience insomnia, too, but that sleeplessness would be tinged with pleasurable excitement. That is why *The Deluxe Transitive Vampire* is addressed to both the eager and the doomed.

Jonquil was anxious about Torquil's response but eager to resume her amorous and cartographic activities in Trajikistan.

anybody / any body, anyone / any one

🍂 *Anybody* and *anyone* are indefinite pronouns. When either of these is not your intended subject or object, allow a space to interfere after *any* in your questions and statements, as exemplified below by Timofey's lascivious *monologue intérieur* and the speculation about the alchemy or toxicology of cookies.

"Any body is preferable to this disembodied afterlife," thought Timofey in a moment of nostalgia for his days of concupiscent cruising.

"Has anybody called?" asked Loona of her answering machine, with no one else to engage at the moment in a bit of repartee.

Anyone who thinks he has a superior Weltanschauung is summoned to the map room.

Any one of these cookies could be the cache for a precious elixir or a fatal splash of strychnine.

NOTE: *As you see in the examples of Loona's loneliness and the savvy philosopher-cartographer,* anybody *and* anyone *take a singular verb.*

anymore / any more

🍂 *Anymore* is the word to use when speaking of time continuing or coming to an end, somewhat synonymous with *any longer. Any more* is an augmentation of quantity.

Anjula doesn't keep house for monosyllabic mesomorphs anymore.

Does the troll want any more cupcakes for his *petit déjeuner sur l'herbe?*

Why shouldn't I hang out with lycanthropes anymore?

any time / anytime

🍂 *Anytime* is an adverb and behaves accordingly. When you want or need a noun, the two words must separate. The same is true when this notion follows a preposition.

Anytime, anywhere, my little langousta, I will be listening for the brittle scamper of your briny claws.

"Will you ever have any time for me?" asked Timofey of his fetching phantom new acquaintance, an habitué of Eternity from long before his own arrival.

Were you at any time aware of an unearthly presence zigzagging along the crenelations?

awake / awaken / wake
awoke / awakened / woke

⚘ These are all variations on the same arousal from sleep, transitive and intransitive, the last three for the past tense. *Awake* and *awaken* are the forms that are used figuratively, as in the panther's raison d'être here.

The baby dragon awoke from a tantalizing dream smacking his lips with pleasure and mischief, his eyes blinking with wily percipience: a sorceress had been teaching him a curiously delicious language that paralyzed his nanny and shattered his sapphires and awakened in the panther an obsession for protecting the dragons' treasure, allowing them to scuttle freely about the Schloss and spy on the humans' capers.

"Will you wake me when it's all over?" Miranda asked the sandman, just to make him believe she was succumbing.

awhile / a while

🔏 *Awhile* is an adverb. To invoke a sense of time as a substance that is fractured or clocked, you might say or write *a while,* a noun, preceded by *for,* just as you say *for an hour, for a few minutes, for weeks on end.*

Will you sit beside my bed and hold my paw awhile till they've removed the leeches?

I'll keep you company for a while if you promise not to let them bind and bleed me.

backward / backwards

🔏 As an adverb, both are correct. As an adjective, only *backward* is.

Stepping and bending backwards, the robot broke the spell of Gardel with a metallic screech.

"Hold your horses! We're rolling backward!" cautioned the conductor, coming to his other senses and tossing aside, with wanton abandon, his naughty magazine.

With a backward glance at her gagged and bound captors (hardly necessary, but she'd wanted to try out a few knots her

daughter had learned at summer camp),
she made a hasty sign of the cross and
flew out the open window through the
lightening sky to crash into her coffin
by sunrise.

barely

🦇 Since *barely* is on the brink of being negative in meaning, preceding it with *not* constitutes a faux pas, as well as a double negative.

not:
He couldn't barely resist her with that tattoo of the
Cheshire cat on her limpid mug.

but:
He could barely resist her with that tattoo of the Cheshire cat
on her limpid mug.

not:
We aren't barely scratching the surface of this touchy,
ticklish subject.

but:
We're barely scratching the surface of this touchy, ticklish
subject.

The banditti barely had time to tiptoe past the pantry and try
two false walls before being assailed by the slinking sentry.

beside / besides

❧ *Beside* means at the side of, while *besides* means in addition to.

"I was beside myself with belief!" cried Jacaranda, recounting the reappearance (and much altered appearance) of her uncle from Trajikistan.

She laid her gloves beside him and placed her torso in his paws.

Besides the suicide bomber, five she-goats, two flashers, and one baby dragon still in its christening gown were killed or mangled in the tragedy at Amplochacha's cathedral.

Miranda was seated beside Mrs. Gallimauf when a rat scampered in wearing a birthday cake, bangles winking on its ankles, a raffish bow on its tail.

"I'm fed up with your fashion fetishes, your lofty airs, your little ways. Besides, I think I'm pregnant by the butler, and we've exchanged vows of eternal adoration over croissants and a relief map of the bottomless lake," said the general factotum of the Schloss, handing in her resignation to her narcissistic mistress.

best

not:
You've got to walk into that chamber of horrors as best prepared as possible, for there's little time to reflect once you're there, face to face with fear.

but:
You've got to walk into that chamber of horrors as well prepared as possible.

You must do the best that you can, and if you are terrorized into closing your eyes, try keeping your wits about you, your sixth sense on the qui vive.

☙ Ampersand suggests that the misexpression *as best as* arises from combining the idea *as well as* with that of doing the best one can: essentially, the two expressions mated and produced a minor monster. As Ampersand points out in explaining why *as best as* is a faux pas, you wouldn't say "She's looking as prettiest as a picture, and as prettiest as she can be." What we have is a compounded comparison/superlative in these errors, a redundancy: choose one or the other, and either will do, even when the comparison is with oneself, one's capacity. Platgut skids into this paragraph, though, to defend the perfectly viable expression "as best you can." Turn the page as best you can and we'll proceed to Montenegro.

biannual / biennial

༭ *Biannual,* like *semiannual,* means twice a year. *Biennial* means every two years.

Late with her biannual dues once again, Miranda was barred from the next symposium, which was to be held at Hotel Artaud.

Our biennial tryst in Venice does not coincide with that city's biennial art festival but with the one in Cetinje, Montenegro.

NOTE: *Think of that first sentence about Miranda's exile as a fore-shadowing of* that / which. *The nonrestrictive clause begins with* which *because we already know it's the next symposium, and the fact that Hotel Artaud shall serve as its venue is incidental, notwithstanding all the frissons that name might produce in Francophiles and dra-maturges.*

biweekly / semiweekly

༭ As you might divine from the above exposition, *biweekly* means every other week, every two weeks; *semiweekly* means twice a week.

Those biweekly effusions in the Gallimaufs' parlor left Miranda and Jacaranda longing for the men of their dreams, and on the prowl to find them. No street, therefore, was safe for anyone in pants on a semimonthly basis. Semiweekly sessions at Blotto Junction placed women in similar peril, however, and often the twain did meet.

both

‡ *Both* is one gadabout that attaches itself anywhere it pleases, unless you take it by the hand and place it beside the word it modifies. Notice the difference in placement of *both* among the nouns and verbs of these two sentences.

I both consider it an honor and regard it as a duty to tend the mustache on the king's statue.

I consider it both an honor and a pleasure to tend the mustache on the king's statue.

‡ Here, the faux pas versions would read:

I both consider it an honor and a duty to tend the mustache on the king's statue.

I consider it both an honor and regard it as a pleasure to tend the mustache on the king's statue.

celebrant / celebrator

☆ Vargas Scronx, partial to ritual and all its mysteries, cautions us to reserve *celebrant* for a priest, priestess, or other person invested with sacred authority who is performing religious rites. Drat Siltlow, who celebrated his twenty-first birthday at a Boston bacchanal, says he was not the only *celebrator* there.

"That minotaur will not do as a celebrant for even one Sunday," mimed the more dogmatic marionettes frantically as the substitute continued with his crude choreography of the Mass and the missing priest celebrated his own saint's day with a toast and a piece of *gâteau de fée* at the Miniature Café.

The Schloss is not averse to celebrators; indeed, it attracts them like a magnet from over the border as well. Dolorous processions have arrived from Trajikistan with no clue as to how this displacement was effected, but with an urgent desire for the *grands crus* in its wine cellar, the Grand Marnier in its soufflés, and the hanky-panky in its boudoirs and bedrooms.

cherubic / seraphic

☆ *Cherubic,* meaning cherub-like, can imply a babylike or childlike plumpness typical of those flying children with chubby faces: toddlers on the wing, in fact. Cherubs form the second order of angels. Seraphs belong to the highest order, and *seraphic,* when applied to a smile, carries more bliss than *cherubic*. The seraph sometimes appears in art as a sweet child's head with wings.

The cherubic, rumpled curator of the Immergau Museum took a holiday in the remotest mountains of Trajikistan and returned svelte and debonair.

Somehow, that seraphic smile seems duplicitous on the mesmerizing mug of the lamia.

The cherubic contingency arrived at the convocation in high spirits, batting their wings in time to an inaudible cha-cha and stealing the shoes of several officious personages at the head of the table and among the official greeting party receiving latecomers at the door.

The chairman's famous seraphic comportment was marred on this occasion by a show of distemper when he had to pad through the ceremony in his not quite up to snuff socks.

childish / childlike

☙ *Childish* is a rebuke, stigma, or aspersion, just one cut above *infantile*. *Childlike* refers to the qualities of childhood worth emulating, or not losing in the first place, which might include innocence, simplicity, guilelessness, artistic inspiration, freedom from affectations, social formalities, and debutante polishings.

In some ways, Sonja Tweazle Scronx was the ideal nanny for the baby dragons, however inadvertently she had adopted this métier. She was proficient in massage and Kung Fu, childlike in her spontaneity and sweetness, discreet about the au pair's secret *sorties,* and accomplished as a soprano and lutanist, the latter distinction initially a boon for the lullabies at nap time, and later for the youngsters' lessons on percussion, harp, and saxophone.

"You're just being childish, Torquil!" said Jonquil, regarding his jealous tantrum (in front of the relics, yet!) with disgust after her confession about the trek in Trajikistan.

collectors' item

꙾ It's not *collector's item.*

"That pram is quite a collectors' item," remarked a passerby in admiration, without the slightest notion of the lovesick potions and makeshift emotions rolling down the avenida with it.

compared to / compared with

> ❧ *Compared to* is used to assert, without further elaboration, that two or more items are similar.

Alyosha compared her crush on the dragon to the torch that W. B. Yeats carried for Maud Gonne.

> ❧ *Compared with* is the combination to use in juxtaposing two or more items to show similarities and/or differences.

The average rainfall in Azuriko is twenty-two inches, compared with the eighty-eight inches that sent the rivers on a rampage in 1895.

The contessa's hair was a fiery gold compared with the marchesa's locks of molten lead.

NOTE: Contrasted to *and* contrasted with *obey a similar pattern.*

compliment / complement

ꕤ *Compliment* is a noun or verb conveying praise. *Complement* is a noun or verb with the notion of completeness, or of balancing or supplementing something.

I'd be wary of such smarmy compliments, if I were you: think of how he carried on about Dante Kaputo's "milkmaid manners" and "the Platguttian grace."

Mucho Trabajo felt sure, or at times merely hoped, that a liaison with a randy lady donkey would complement his manifold humiliations and iniquitous servitude.

"Compliments to the chef, and ask him to whip up another!" said Dragomir, still puzzled by the enigmatic *arrière-goût* of the sous-chef's soufflé.

comport / consort

☙ *Comport* means to conduct or behave oneself in a particular manner.

"Comport yourself with more docility—or decorum, anyway—young lady, or we'll throw you overboard," said the skipper of the *Scarlatina* as it shattered the Sargasso Sea.

☙ *Consort* as a verb means to associate, to keep company.

"I shall consort with whomever I wish and in whatever manner I please!" retorted the headstrong second mate, Ziggie Spurthrast, who had taken quite a fancy to most of the passengers and sabotaged the sous-chef's soirée by cooking a clog in his soufflé.

☙ As a singular noun, *consort* means companion, partner, lover, husband, wife; it's often used for the spouse of a monarch. The collective noun means group, company, such as an ensemble of musicians.

At the death of the royal consort, musical consorts throughout the land played dirges, and the city of Amplochacha was draped in mourning—even the horses drawing state coaches wore black bands on their forequarters—while twenty supplementary scribes were taken on to handle the letters of condolence addressed to King Alabastro, who could not be talked out of the mousseline pajamas he'd been wearing when his beloved queen, Dariushka, died of fright in her sleep.

compose / comprise

֍ *Compose* means to create, put together, assemble, and re-joices in both active and passive employment.

Constanza was composing her memoir of how maddeningly life and art mirrored each other while she was singing the adulterous role of Tereza Terrazzo in *La Inclemenza di Signora Rastito* at Duque de Caxias.

It is composed of some mysterious substance that seems to bend and stiffen at will.

֍ *Comprise* means to include all of, encompass, embrace, contain, and is on its best behavior in active voice with a direct object following.

The botanical gardens comprise a frightening collection of voracious violets simulating shyness and dejected dahlias feigning mirth.

The Velveteen Rabble, an opera composed by Whiffle Clackengirth, comprises fifty acts, each one requiring a change of scene and a change of the audience's costumes.

condole / console

֍ We are in the Slough of Despond here, with only a couple of verbs to save us.

☙ *Condole* is usually accompanied by *with,* and means to express one's sympathy or condolences to someone who is suffering grief, sorrow, misfortune. *Console* is a transitive verb meaning to lessen or soften someone's pain, loss, misfortune, sorrow, to give solace or comfort.

I condole with you, I really do, however reluctantly you receive me, and I will go on condoling with you however you disbelieve me.

Nothing I tried seemed to assuage his sufferings: I utterly failed to console him. I enjoined his friends to deluge him with frivolous gifts, tender notes, lascivious suggestions, to kiss his knuckles and pat his shoulder, but all was to no avail, and we finally abandoned Count Ghastly to his dirge and oversized hankies, his moues and self-flagellations.

—*The Wretch of Lugubria*

consist in / consist of

☙ *Consist in* means to lie in or inhere in, to have as a defining attribute. *Consist of* means to be composed of.

"Solipsism," lectured Strophe Dulac, "consists in leaving the self untouched."

The lamia's false allure consists in her borrowed trappings.

The baby dragons' mid-morning snack usually consists of water hot from the geyser with crushed rubies and a drop of gold; *crèpes chaussettes* with rose petal jam; sautéed tails of mermaid teenagers; aquavit; pulverized albino python bones; broth of salamander with caviar toasts; and ice cream with essence of petrol.

couple

🔧 Never castrate *couple* of its preposition *of* when it's enumerating.

not:
"Gimme a couple blindfolds now we've got their ankles and wrists calmed down," said the brunette brigand to the blond.

but:
"I'll have a couple of blokes with this pint of ale," said Cassandra, sizing up several tables of louts.

NOTE: *Use a plural verb when such a construction is in action.*

A couple of louts were on the make, a couple of them were on the lam.

We came across a couple of hermits on a crag in Trajikistan who were having a spat about a species of serpent that once terrorized their garrulous brook and its wayfarers.

⅄ See also the Agreements chapter of *The Deluxe Transitive Vampire,* where *couple* and *pair* are considered under collective nouns.

dangling participles

⅄ Participles dangle when they are not attached to the word they modify, and sometimes that word is nowhere in sight. So do participial, infinitive, gerund, and prepositional phrases, as well as elliptical clauses. We will consider the matter blithely and briefly here, and pursue it to the ends of the earth (well, all the way to Trajikistan) later.

⅄ Dangling participles can often be redressed by changing the subject of the sentence, as these fleeting visits to a ballroom and a slumber party remind us.

Overwhelmed, the ballroom was spinning around her as the debutante panted and tried to catch her breath.

⅄ Since it was the debutante and not the ballroom that was overwhelmed, the elements of this sentence must dance into new places:

Overwhelmed, the debutante panted and tried to catch her breath, the ballroom spinning around her.

or:

With the ballroom spinning around her, the overwhelmed debutante panted and tried to catch her breath.

dangling participial phrase

Yowling like cats as the girls tore into their presents, the floor was a heap of ribbons and disarray.

ꝏ rearranged with subject in its place, the subject being "the girls":

Yowling like cats as they tore into their presents, the girls turned the floor into a heap of ribbons and disarray.

ꝏ It is because of how the sentence is set up, its architecture, that "the girls" must follow the comma, that pause after the participial phrase. Even though the girls are present in the phrase itself, the subject ("girls") belonging to the participle must be where "the floor" mistakenly is in the first example. Everything in the first half is signaling that the subject is about to appear, and the subject is not "the floor," which is not yowling. In this example, the birthday is caterwauling and guzzling:

Carbonating their muscles with cheap champagne and caterwauling as they rolled on the floor, the birthday became a bacchanalian bazaar.

rearranged:
With the girls caterwauling, carbonating their muscles with cheap champagne, and rolling on the floor, the birthday became a bacchanalian bazaar.

᠅ Lest the subject make you fling this book down so soon in despair and dejection, I have banished dangling particip-ial phrases and their fellow criminals to their own iniquitous ghetto, which you may reach by going past the end of the al-phabet to Perilous Phrases or riffling through the index. Forgetting he'd summoned his other half midway through the composition of *Semi-detached Constructions,* a monograph on misplacements, Natty Ampersand committed suicide (by hanging, of course, and the noose was made of particip-ial, infinitive, and gerund phrases he'd been tangling with for the previous three weeks) and left the work unfinished. It's the one I have consulted, nevertheless. Although he was buried in the same cemetery as Timofey, he wasn't quite finished off! His female self was answering his summons just as his legs gave their last jerk (considering the nature of his despondency, it would be tasteless to insist on his erection), and this part of him lives on. Natty has changed her name, however, to Nada Seria, and after a spell as amanuensis to a contralto, she now writes romance novels full of social and grammatical faux pas. No longer threatened with sexual identity crises, she even married Monsieur Joubert Plume and has birthed several cherubim of her own.

different from / different than

🍂 In most comparisons, *different from* is the combination to use, if there is a difference.

The rat in the Mickey Mouse T-shirt is different from the one whose mug shot is such an amusing addition to our files.

🍂 *Different than* is correct when the comparison is completed by a clause with a verb in it.

The dénouement of *The Stupor of Flanelle Lune* was different than we expected it to be. Not only did the protagonist get her comeuppance, but she also shrugged off her pajamas and arose from her bed.

"This honeymoon is different from the last one I had," said Laurinda as the tracers filigreed the night sky.

"This honeymoon is different than I imagined it would be—well, the background, anyway," she wrote on a post card to her uncle.

double negative

🍂 A double negative is not to be avoided so much because two "no's" make a "yes" (and misunderstandings, and misbehavior based on them, would follow) as because it's fallen out of fashion since the days of Chaucer, the Churl Poet, and Shakespeare, when it thrived in many expressions and combinations. When you get past these examples you will come to a clearing (brook babbling in the near distance: watch out for fauns and nymphs) where the exaltation of double negatives holds sway. Meanwhile, the double negative is fine for colloquial talk over platters of crawfish or Cajun torch songs, but in prose meant to convince, inform, seduce, expostulate, it's best to knowingly leave out one negative or the other, as in the alternatives offered after each of the following faux pas. Did you remark that I have just knowingly and jubilantly split an infinitive?

not:
"I haven't seen nobody besides a broken cellist pass this way since sundown," said the chappie two miles down the dusty road from the hacienda.

but:
I haven't seen anyone besides a broken cellist pass this way since sundown.

not:
"I'm not never going to sign up for one of those displeasure cruises," protested the dummy in the the arms of Anja at the Trajikistan travel bureau.

but:
"I'm not ever going to sign up for one of those displeasure cruises," protested the dummy in the the arms of Anja at the Trajikistan travel bureau.

or:
I won't ever sign up for one of those displeasure cruises.
I'm never going to sign up for one of those displeasure cruises.

not:
It didn't make no sense to the debutante that her life should have started at all.

but:
It didn't make any sense to the debutante that her life should have started at all.

It made no sense to the debutante that her life should have started at all.

not:
I wasn't doing nothing when that samovar suddenly exploded.

but:
I wasn't doing anything when that samovar suddenly exploded.

or:
I was doing nothing at all when that samovar suddenly exploded.

<u>**NOTE:**</u> *See also* barely, hardly, scarcely.

✦ *Whether* sometimes doubles its *nots* in a misguided play for emphasis.

not:

Whether or not the Schloss would still be standing or not was a matter of dire uncertainty during the reign of Alabastro II.

but:

Whether or not the Schloss would still be standing was a matter of dire uncertainty during the reign of Alabastro II.

᠅ See also *if* / *whether* to further acquaint yourself with these innuendos.

᠅ The double negatives of country and rockabilly music allow for extra syllables to come into play, let other words into the line, and also keep a song line tight, with the obliging "ain't." A mere syllable counts for a lot when you're writing songs or poetry.* "You aren't anything but a hound dog" throws that rhythm off the stage, while "You are nothing but a hound dog" takes the punch out of the put-down so wallopingly conveyed by "You ain't nothin' but a hound dog." Here, the double negative, rather than becoming positive, seems to quadruple the insult (giving it four legs). So, anyway, does Drat Siltlow's argument run, and he has the benefit of the Appalachian Mountains, St. Louis and his mother's blues, and a Harvard education.

* Same thing goes for "He don't have no more fond regard for me," which saves two extra syllables you'd get with "doesn't" and "any." "Ain't" is eminently acceptable in such situations where you'd otherwise have to say "he isn't" and thereby lose one precious syllable you might use much more fascinatingly in the torrid ballad you are wailing.

𝄐 Natty Ampersand
wrote

of having decapitated several lovers for miffing her upon her return to the female sex with the greeting: "I've missed not seeing you." As Natty pointed out, with poised scimitar, what they were really saying was they missed her absence or invisibility and could hardly wait for her to disappear again, and she'd only just arrived! What should they have said, had they valued their lives—or their heads? Either "I've missed you" or "I've missed seeing you," the latter really a rather lame declaration of fact: you've been invisible to me, or I have not seen you. Startling Glower encountered the same quasi-double negative from several critics and fans of his theatrical career upon his opening with a new play. He'd greet these statements with Congrevous ripostes such as "And I've not missed not avoiding your bêtises."

𝄐 Vargas Scronx holds forth on a related instance of faulty logic as he scrutinizes the expression "I couldn't care less," an expression of supreme indifference, which is sometimes misfashioned into "I could care less" which means not at all the same thing. It could, in fact, mean one cares very much, or cares to some extent, anyway.

𝄐 Meanwhile, back in the bureaucracy, the double negative has underhanded, disingenuous purposes of other persuasions. Just the sort of flummery or bombast in which such confutations as *irregardless* and *disabuse* abound! A brilliant example from academia occurs in Stephen Fry's *The Liar,* in which Tim Anderson speaks a language that is the only Modern European language that Professor Donald Trefusis has failed to learn or comprehend:

"Well that's a not uninteresting point, certainly," said Anderson, "but I was thinking more that I don't know many people who couldn't express doubt about the strategies that the authorities adopt in situations not a million miles dissimilar to this one and I just don't think that's something we shouldn't be unafraid to shirk addressing or confronting."

doubt

⸓ *Doubt* should not be snagged into an awkward construction by an unnecessary subsequent *but that.*

not:
I have no doubt but that I'm the one you want, with my creamy curriculum vitae and my flinty aplomb.

but:
I have no doubt that I'm the one you want, with my creamy curriculum vitae and my flinty aplomb.

We have no doubt that you're hot stuff; however, it's mediocrity and mendacity that make our company tick.

≯· *Doubt that,* not *doubt if,* is the expression to use in negative or interrogative sentences when little doubt exists, as in the above interview and the following sentence. *Doubt whether* is for expressing strong uncertainty.

I doubt that I'll find time for you and your lamentations between now and Epiphany.

I doubt whether the parliament of Azuriko will survive this river's rages; it's a very efficient system of government rejuvenation.

dudgeon / dungeon

≯· "In high dudgeon" is such an offended, resentful, indignant state of mind that it is evident, even if the angered party has no tail to thrash: other body language will suffice.

≯· Aelfric Valinthrob, having once spent some time in a dungeon (his wife locked him in it back when she was his pet grad student and he was still writing his dissertation himself—the reason for his imprisonment), came out of it in high dudgeon, and has remained so ever since. Neither should *dudgeon* be confused with "donjon," the inner keep of a castle in Medieval France, nor with Don Juan, a menace in pants.

each other / one another

🔸 *Each other* is apt when the exchange is between two people or some other giving and receiving duo. Once upon a time, *one another* was used more consistently than it now is when more than two were concerned. These days, it is still preferred for three or more, but it can also apply to an exchange involving two persons or other beings.

We sang to one another our favorite country hits: "Blaze On, My Little Tumbleweed," "Alabaster Highway," and "We Had a Continental Breakfast Kind of Love."

For their first wedding anniversary, they gave each other paper hats and paper pajamas on which to write reckless recriminations, wacky endearments, impossible promises, and ribald requests.

elicit / illicit

🪶 *Elicit* means to call forth or invite.

🪶 *Illicit* means unlawful, prohibited.

Amaranthia's procession of motorcycles to the mausoleum elicited reprehension from the organist and commendation from the priest.

Illicit trade on the waterways of Azuriko continued not only unimpeded but abetted by the floods: barges of uprooted families and photo albums camouflaged pornographic postage stamps; drowning puppies and floating televisions harbored Ziplocked substances with uncertain effects; and valiant rescuers unwittingly transported messages to the exiled duchess grinding her rubies and pawning her diadems and wedding rings so that the monarchists in Lavukistan could run their magazine and straighten their teeth.

elliptical clauses

🪶 Elliptical clauses, like perilous phrases, can derange your sentences when you allow them to dangle just as your sentence is getting under way. In an elliptical clause, one or more missing words are understood. It's usually the subject, and sometimes part of the verb, that we sense between the words. In the first example we understand that it was *she* who was but a little wraith during her necromantic apprenticeship, and not the hoary old alchemist (even if he/she may have been a wraith once upon a time). The dangling comes in where the main narrative of the sentence takes over, in which a new and different subject is suddenly doing what the implied subject of the elliptical clause should be doing if it were dancing with the structure already in full swing. As Platgut puts it: Unless the implied or understood subject is the same as that of the main clause, the elliptical clause will dangle.

dangling:
While but a little wraith of a sorceress, a hoary old alchemist taught her many spells and curses she was to boggle later in life.

　※ As it was not the alchemist, but *she* who was once a little wraith, the words must be shifted.

right:
While but a little wraith of a sorceress, she was taught by a hoary old alchemist many spells and curses she was to boggle later in life.

even more apropos:
While but a little wraith of a sorceress, she learned from a hoary old alchemist many spells and curses she was to boggle later in life.

caution:
While but a little wraith of a sorceress, she learned many spells and curses from a hoary old alchemist she was to boggle later in life.

NOTE: *In this last example, a misplaced phrase finds her boggling the alchemist, and not his nefarious curriculum.*

dangling:
When a cherub of four years old, her uncle would put things in his pipe and smoke them as she bounced upon his knee.

right:
When she was a cherub of four years old, her uncle would put things in his pipe and smoke them as she bounced upon his knee.

right:
When a cherub of four years old, she would bounce upon her uncle's knee as he put things in his pipe and smoked them.

dangling:
When not yet past the portals of puberty, her podiatrist pounced on her.

right:
When not yet past the portals of puberty, she was pounced on by her podiatrist.

dangling:
Although holding forth flamboyantly and flashing his brightened teeth, his audience was crushed with ennui.

right:
Although holding forth flamboyantly and flashing his brightened teeth, he was crushing his audience with ennui.

dangling:
After ransacking the roadhouse on the eve of the truce, the

peace pact had fresh grievances to arbitrate, and fresh hot ruffians to shoot.

right:
After the roadhouse had been ransacked on the eve of the truce, the peace pact had fresh grievances to arbitrate, and fresh hot ruffians to shoot.

    🙔 Oxymoronically, the first sentence of this pair has the peace pact itself wreaking havoc.

not:
While sharpening my claws, the tailor rebounded with his scissors.

    🙔 Why not? I was sharpening my claws; he was sharpening his scissors, and did so faster than I. So it should read:

While I was still sharpening my claws, the tailor rebounded with his scissors.

not:
Before cooled to lipsmacking perfection, the little tyrants pounced on the meringues and singed their sophisticated palates.

but:
Before the meringues were cooled to lipsmacking perfection, the little tyrants pounced on them and singed their sophisticated palates.

empirical / empyrean

🔧 *Empirical,* a philosophical term that belongs very much in our everyday life, means derived from or guided by or depending upon experience and observation alone, without scientific verification.

Empirical evidence
suggests that death
is not becoming to the corpse,
however gorgeous the mourner
looks in black.

NOTE: *See* parallel constructions *to follow this line of thought: If I had enslaved myself to strict exigencies of parallel construction, I would have ended up with a less attractive sentence, losing that smacking sound at the end:*

Empirical evidence suggests that death is not becoming to the corpse, however gorgeous black is for the mourner / however gorgeous black makes the mourner.

I have only empirical arguments to offer for my insistence on the existence of life in outer space: I was kidnapped by some such life form and whirled through a tour of its kindergartens, its retirement villas, its Division of Skyways and Tombs.

꠵ *Empyrean* means the highest reaches of heaven, believed in ancient times to be a realm of pure fire or light; the abode of God, paradise; the sky, space. As an adjective, *empyrean* refers to that first, exalted sense, those sublime heights.

"I must tell you that he is a rogue, you can't buy anything in his shop: he puts all kinds of filth into the wine—sandalwood, burnt cork and even elderberry; but if you get a bottle from his back room, the one he calls the 'special,' well then, brother, you are in the empyrean."

—Nikolai Gogol, *Dead Souls*

enormity / enormousness

꠵ *Enormousness* refers to size; *enormity* is about unspeakable horrors, monstrous deeds, cruel and perfidious behavior.

The heinousness of these allegations was eclipsed by the enormity of the brigands' brusque but brutal attack.

The enormousness of the cosmos was nothing beside the voluminous clamor of her love.

We clanged and clamored for our waiter, Torso, to protest the enormousness of the platter, the diminution of the cake.

equally

❧ *Equally* is never followed by *as*. Sometimes it's the *equally* you don't want or need, preferring a comparison including *as*.

not:
We are all equally as beautiful as that upstart from hell.

but:

We are all as beautiful
as that upstart from hell.

We are all equal in beauty
to that upstart from hell.

Light and dark are equally potent on this earth, and although light is often granted supremacy, sometimes shadows are as alluring as a splash of gold or flash of incandescence.

Yes, the performers must sing and play to perfection, but equally important is the audience's grace, dexterity, and dispatch through their fifty costume changes that are an integral part of the opera.

NOTE: *While* audience *may take a singular or plural pronoun depending on the circumstances and its cohesiveness, this audience takes the plural* their *to convey the individual grace, dexterity, and dispatch of its myriad members.*

etc. 

Natty Ampersand puts the matter this way: Because *et cetera,* for which *etc.* is an abbreviation, means "and other things of the same kind," although most of us translate this further into "and so on and so forth," there is never any reason for an *and* to precede this insinuation, which already has one in its mouth. And never mind, she adds, that one does encounter in antiquated novels with epistolary expositions such sign-offs as "Yours & etc., Bottie Whifflecurst." *Etc.* should be used only when it is apparent what "other things of the same kind" might be, or where "so forth" is going. When Startling Glower presented his "Up Your Eponym, etc." program, he went into lurid (and censored) detail as he and his guests improvised on the possibilities of that preposition and possessive pronoun.

Her night shift (she was usually wearing one, too) meant that she left the bakery each day at dawn, her homeward path slithering along his open trenches, her bear claws warring with his toy guns, her croissants with his scimitars, etc.

The Let's Face It beauty parlor, not much to look at, was closed on alternate Tuesdays for waxing the proprietor's legs and mustache, singeing her curls, buffing and lacquering her claws, etc.

even

꘠ *Even* should be placed near the verb it modifies, even if it must thereby jump into the midst of a compound verb.

not:
She even had bought a silver negligee with wings sprouting out of the shoulders, and winged slippers to match.

but:
She had even bought a silver negligee with wings sprouting out of the shoulders, and winged slippers to match.

not:
The slippers even could flap their wings when she tugged a tiny cord on her bustier.

but:
The slippers could even flap their wings when she tugged a tiny cord on her bustier.

everyone / every one

❧ *Everyone* is a big, inclusive pronoun; *every one* nods to individual items and says they all are present and under consideration. Both take a singular verb.

Every one of the broken records has been a hit in its day.

Everyone stranded in the Schloss has shed a few inhibitions.

exalt / exult

❧ *Exalt* is a transitive verb; *exult* is intransitive in action. Someone who exults could be called exultant.

He exalts the solidity of cumbrous furniture over the virtues of pillows and ottomans.

How they exulted as they snatched away the brigands' fans! It was indeed a triumph fit for vaunting.

farther / further

❧ *Farther* refers specifically to measurable distance or space. *Further* encompasses much more, reaching further than its sister with her peripatetic measuring tape. *Further* means greater in degree, quantity, and time.

Timofey's tomb lies five rows farther down the lane that's lined with skulls and lindens.

Let us explore these synchronicities further, and try to identify the point at which this meeting of ours became inevitable.

The plot of *The Stupor of Flanelle Lune* merits further study: the novel may be more than an allegory of anomie or an exposé of narcolepsy.

This nonsense cannot go on any further without a séance of refection and reflection at Café Frangipane.

    ⸎ *Further* is also used as a verb meaning to promote.

Boris Marcelovsky wrestles with the diva's tempestuous tresses for two reasons: he adores the gossip, and her custom furthered his career when he was just an arriviste from the tenebrous wastes of Trajikistan.

fewer / less

    ⸎ As Zoë Platgut succinctly and colloquially declares, *fewer* counts and *less* measures, although a few exceptions occur at the end of this exposition.

Fewer lights are burning in the Schloss tonight because there's an orgy in the *grand salon*.

Less clothing is covering the cavorting bodies than is scattered with the shattered chandelier over the parquet floor.

The baby vampire has made fewer attacks on his playmates this week than he did the last week of October. (It is only after puberty that vampires turn nocturnal in their pursuit of the jugular.)

There's less blood in little Lola's veins since they last played spin the bottle with the lights down low.

NOTE: *Use* less *when the number is only one.*

I received one less threat today than yesterday.

There's one less troubadour on the road since the duel that removed Perceval Longitude.

꠹ Exceptions: Use *less* for quantities of time, distance, weight, and money.

"I'll take five ounces less of the Explorateur this time, three ounces more of the Rocomadour," said the rat to the girl with the ponytail as she pranced about the cheese shop.

The Schloss is less than ten kilometers from the station, which makes it an easy weekend getaway for the rambunctious from Amplochacha.

The butler never needs less than five minutes to shuffle out when the first bars of *Transfigured Night* sound at the front door.

In spite of his lugubrious manner, no guest ever leaves the little butler less than fifteen zlotky in tips—and twice that for the massive maids.

꜔ Cram Fossilblast, in romantic reverie, insists this too is an exception, but, true to his romanticism, refuses to give a reason:

The usual declaration of love in English requires no less than three words.

flaunt / flout

꜔ *Flaunt* means to show off, to make a boastful or ostentatious display. *Flout* means to scoff at, to mock, scorn.

Flouting the decorum of their slim, prim elders in overstuffed chairs, the gaudy, baubled offspring of this solemn community cut careening, flamboyant swathes up its sober streets and down its placid lanes. Bedizened in ribbons, lace, and satin elbow patches, even the young men flaunted sartorial impudence and eye-shadowed their sockets in motley hues.
—*The Lambkins of Dreadmore Valley*

The pastry chef flaunted his strange new creations: *crème passionnelle, napoléon à la Russe* (a total disaster), and the illusory *gâteau de fée.*

Sisyphus is still flouting the law of gravity—or trying to, anyway.

fragments

❧ *The Deluxe Transitive Vampire* sups voluptuously on the blood of several fragments, but I couldn't help presenting some of the fragmented dialogue from "Up Your Eponym"—faux fragments, that is, for our written and spoken intercourse gives us occasion to splutter incomplete sentences whose meanings are nevertheless full, understood, rounded out by the repartee.

Never!
Just around the corner.
And here, of all places!
Well, upon my soul!
The spitting image of his faux papa!
Why ever not?
Trussed up like a Lazarus on the town!
Oh, hell!
You low-down lying scamp.
And how!
My God, the cake!
What a crushing afternoon!
Off her bloody rocker!
Up yours, too!

hardly

❧ Since *hardly* is diminishing or dismissive enough to be negative in meaning, doubling it up with *not* undoes the disparaging intention.

not:

I couldn't hardly gild the lily with what was left in my pocket after that tour of Bosoxia.

but:
I could hardly gild the lily with what was left in my pocket after that tour of Bosoxia.

not:

She couldn't hardly blame her firm, upstanding mother for having spawned such a supple, scattered sorceress.

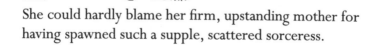

but:
She could hardly blame her firm, upstanding mother for having spawned such a supple, scattered sorceress.

not:

This isn't hardly the place to be discussing such a riveting and intricate conundrum.

but:
This is hardly the place to be discussing such a riveting and intricate conundrum.

⁊ Aelfric Valinthrob yanks a knight out of one of his jousting tournaments to illuminate this issue too:

not:
He couldn't hardly clamber atop his charger with that clanking, cumbrous, rusted armor impeding his every jerk, stretch, and twitch.

but:
He could hardly clamber atop his charger with that clanking, cumbrous, rusted armor impeding his every jerk, stretch, and twitch.

NOTE: Hardly *is also sometimes followed by* none *or* no, *a similarly faulty and ineffective construction:* hardly none *of the cake was left,* hardly no *words of the song remembered could be recast as* almost none *or* hardly any *of the cake;* hardly any *or* very few *of the words of the song.* Scarcely *takes the same cake—I mean treatment.*

hardly than / hardly when

⁊ Since in this construction the relationship is a matter of time, *when,* being more logical, is preferable.

not:
The orgy had hardly gotten under way than a terrific clap of thunder sent a shudder through the entangled torsos and limbs.

but:

The orgy had hardly gotten under way when a terrific clap of thunder sent a shudder through the entangled torsos and limbs.

not:

She'd hardly removed her gloves and stockings than it was time to button her blouse again and rout about in her reticule.

but:

She'd hardly removed her gloves and stockings when it was time to button her blouse again and rout about in her reticule.

if / whether

❧ *If* is used colloquially sometimes where *whether* might otherwise belong. *Whether* is particularly called for in such expressions as *doubt whether, learn whether, know whether, see whether.* Furthermore, *whether* is the word to use when *or not* follows it (even unstated or implied) and when it's introducing more than one condition.

Find out whether or not this anodyne has been patented, and while you're at it, you might also inquire whether it's killed anyone besides that careless maid and the unfortunate panther.

"I doubt whether he'll be needing these where he's going, but he asked to be buried with them all the same," said Nadia, tucking her red boots into his coffin before it was locked, lowered, and showered with handfuls of terra firma.

The organist asked whether she had been a Hungarian dancer or had procured the boots while tramping through Budapest as a free-world agent.

immanent / imminent

⸾· *Imminent* means about to happen, coming soon.

As we sensed the dénouement was imminent, we roused the heroine of *Torpor in the Swing* so she wouldn't miss her startling final chapter.

⸾· You'll probably have less use for *immanent,* unless you're living in a pantheistic or Rococo dream. It means inherent, indwelling, inhabiting, remaining within, and is often applied to spiritual matters.

Demonic forces and nefarious spirits were immanent long before the first kinky despot racked and ruined the land of Blegue.

imply / infer

❧ An interlocutor or a reading or listening audience *infers* something from the words that the speaker or writer *implies*.

But when you offered me a job in the map room, you implied that I'd soon be on my way to the lands delineated in its drawers. I inferred that a series of perilous adventures awaited me:
serpents with wings
slithering out of rose bushes;
banditti in boleros telling my fortune with cards;
penguins in Patagonia taking my orders at roadside cafés;
slumber parties with lycanthropes smoking cigarettes;
and refugees from rejected realms sketching out new
territories to which we'd all escape.

incomplete comparisons

incomplete:
The allure of sirens who are impostors is less
than real ones.

rightly rounded off:
The allure of sirens who are impostors is less
than that of real ones.

incomplete:
Please continue. These anecdotes of yours are more
entertaining than most travelers I've met on rackety trains.

complete:
Please continue. These anecdotes of yours are more
entertaining than those of most travelers I've met on
rackety trains.

> ⸘ Parallel construction is something to keep in mind with
> these comparisons; remember this when we hit that con-
> struction zone.

incomplete:
The endangered species of Bosoxia are different
from Azuriko.

complete:
The endangered species of Bosoxia are different
from those of Azuriko.

incomplete:
The terrain of eastern Lavukistan is different from western
Louvelandia.

complete:
The terrain of eastern Lavukistan is different from that of
western Louvelandia.

ineffable / unspeakable

    ❧ *Ineffable* conveys the idea of something no words can ex-
press because it's too splendidly, deliciously indescribable.

Unspeakable applies to things so vile, outrageous, offensive that they are difficult or revolting to talk about, inexpressibly horrendous.

The ineffable pleasures invoked by these visions surrendered to acute chagrin when I found myself a mere minion charting the restive borderlands where unspeakable atrocities provoked unconscionable retaliations between one truculent tribe and another.

ingenious / ingenuous

𝄃· For *ingenious,* think of *genius;* for *ingenuous, ingenue.* *Ingenious* means remarkably clever; *ingenuous* means innocent, naïve, without guile.

They figured out an ingenious way of floating the contraband down the river without detection. The crew wore antlers, the brigands got their fans into furious motion, and the impression was altogether so disarming that no one thought to look past it.

"I may be nubile and defenseless, but I am not ingenuous," adumbrated Jesperanda as a prelude to her anecdote about a naughty amphora.

inhuman / unhuman

❧ The meaning of *inhuman*—brutal, cruel—rests on the notion of humankind as innately good, kind, and just. *Unhuman* means not human, so it could apply to innocuous phantoms, taunting banshees, tiger angels, the songs of sirens.

These rapes, tortures, and other inhuman excesses are inflicting injury on the borderlands' tourist trade as well as on their terrorized inhabitants.

Azuriko relies on unhuman forces to clear the way for new blood and brains in its governing bodies.

inimical / inimitable

❧ *Inimical* has an enemy in it, whether it applies to a look, a feeling, a policy, a gesture, an expulsion, an attack, a scrap of gossip: unfriendly, hostile. Conditions that are inimical are unfavorable, harmful, adverse.

The generalissimo couldn't count on the mercenaries' being inimical enough to wreak the havoc on which he was so intent.

The climate in southern Lavukistan is inimical to hot flashers: that's why she's rented a pavilion for her holidays in fair blue Azuriko.

꙳ Something that is *inimitable* cannot be imitated.

She gave him one of her inimitable looks that said, "Come into my confidence and froufrou, but leave your braggadocio at the door."

irregardless

꙳ Disregard this tautology forever and use *regardless* instead.

its / it's

꙳ When *it* possesses, it does so with *its*. When you're in a hurry to say *it is,* you might commandeer an *it's*. *It's* is also a contraction for *it has,* as in the first colloquially worded bit of dialogue.

"It's got a cinder in its paw, and its whimpers can be heard all the way to hell, the probable provenance of that tormenting grit," cautioned the vet, who'd seen several cases of netherworld inflictions among his feline patients.

"It's not the first time I've come home to find you flicking ashes on my cloud," said the tall svelte angel they called Cindrael, in charge of chastising cherubim caught with cigarettes, chewing gum, and other abusive substances.

It's not what you think! I was only stopping by to predict the weather and ask if that creature had emerged from its cocoon, dispelling the enigma that's held you in thrall for these many weeks.

lend / loan

🔆 A *loan* is what you grant to another or what he blows on a spree. *Lend* is the verb by means of which this money gets into his hands or hers.

Lend me your beauty, your brains, your Bugatti.

The loan of her brains could not be arranged, but I made off with her cleavage and false nails.

The Bugatti, already on loan to the girl next door, lent a glitter to her careening course.

What Polonius would have made of all these transactions was the subject of their fathers' convocations through the long June nights that year. They spent an entire week lending each other their ears and knocking back bourbon and gin.

lie / lay

⚜ *Lie* is intransitive, while *lay* is transitive. Zoë Platgut floored several exercise instructors for telling their students to "lay down" or "lay on your side." The instructors had started out standing up, but Zoë had them decked in seconds and took over the classes herself, suggesting that if those mesomorphs couldn't master such distinctions, they switch the command to "Stretch it out."

Just lie there, Timofey, and pretend you're dead.

Timofey once lay on a feather bed; now he lies buried in the family plot among ancient heroes of Trajikistan.

Don't lay down your troubles in my cognizance, or I'll really give you something to cry about.

⚜ *Laid* is the past tense of *lay*.

She laid it on the table and beat it.

⚜ *Lay* is also the past tense of *lie*, as we saw above in the Timofey flashback and see below in this concupiscent pastorale:

The burden of proof lay with Mucho Trabajo, who'd been taking a siesta at the time. He was dreaming of how he'd couple with a bedroom-eyed donkey; in this vision, they lay together in his pasture, having munched a bit of post-coital grass together and nuzzled each other with flared nostrils, their breath softening as their heartbeats slowed down and the afterglow of love suffused them along with the late afternoon sun.

light

❧ When the verb *to light* slips into the past tense, it does so in the usual way: *lighted*. Sometimes *lit,* also acceptable, sounds better in a given context.

He lighted my fire.
I lit his cigar.

❧ *Lit* is a more colloquial version, and is the more likely choice when one is *lighting out* (setting out, striking out) for a destination, since this is an idiomatic expression. The same is true of the other colloquial use overheard about the following bellicose incident at the Pink Antler Saloon:

"Dante Kaputo lit into Rafael Todos los Muertos at the bar, dragged him into the powder room (where a transvestite barmaid was touching up his face), and KO'd him on the floor of the loo," said Angie Canasta to her coiffeur.

🜚 *Light* also means to descend or land, and with this meaning, too, either *lighted* or *lit* will take you into the past.

The bat lit briefly on Loona's head before flitting off to find its mate.

like / as

🜚 "Do as I say, not as I do," said Cram Fossilblast to me while we trysted at a trattoria—although he was later to amend this to "Do as I write, not as I speak," since spoken language is more indulgent toward the informal use of *like* as a conjunction, a use that goes back centuries. Indeed, exaggerated obedience to this rule (it's coming!) can lead to outright blunders, as I discovered the night "Up Your Eponym" invaded my boudoir and forced me to play parlor games with words drawn out of a mad hatter's hip pocket: these two were my downfall. Bewitched by the savage allure of my native Louvelandia, Startling Glower stayed on and sorted things out for me.

🜚 The conservative camp puts it like this: *Like* should not be used as a conjunction before a subordinate clause containing a verb; such comparisons should begin with *as*.

You're beating your wings against the firmament just as we're rubbing our flanks on the planks.

Alyosha dazed the dragon with her camera much as she once galvanized gargoyles with her velvet glove.

What am I doing?! I'm waiting for Godot, as are those garrulous *clochards*.

⅄ However, *like* is often used in such instances, as a conjunction introducing a clause, and is not universally condemned for such behavior:

That Bugatti roared down the street like it used to before the accident.

⅄ Overzealous during "Up Your Eponym," I found myself using *as* where *like* really should have been, in such statements as "the wolves howl as the hounds of hell" and "this schnapps tastes as fermented mare's milk," when *like* was the correct choice. *As* does belong in the following construction, since *like* should not be used interchangeably for *as if*:

My schnapps tastes as if it's been tampered with by someone in this room.

⅄ Here, *like* correctly precedes a noun or pronoun, in written language as well as the vernacular:

That flick of the dragon's tail works like a charm every time, especially when he bats his eyes and snorts a cloud of scented smoke.

Isn't it just like her, though, to take up with a beast on fire after effacing fifty gargoyles' features with her ceaseless caresses.

loath / loathe

🔑 *Loath* is an adjective meaning hesitant, reluctant, unwilling, and the ending sound is like the beginning of *think*. *To loathe* is to dislike intensely, hate, despise, abhor; the ending sound is like the beginning of *there*.

"I wouldn't be loath to join you in Buenos Aires if you can get past airport security with all that metal in your bones," professed the dentist to the robot several tangos after the robot's romantic proposal.

"I loathe the name I was given: that's why I'm taking a new one," announced Incognito I when he was still Crown Prince ———— (royal edict prohibits us from pronouncing the forsaken word).

luxuriant / luxurious

🔑 *Luxuriant* means growing profusely, as in a garden luxuriant with fiddlehead ferns, foxglove, and tuberose. *Luxurious* refers to riches, displays or feelings of wealth: characterized by or given to luxury.

Among the wraps in the cloakroom were a muff of luxuriant fox fur and a raccoon-collared vest discussing the libretto of *La Inclemenza di Signora Rastito* and the contralto's infamous trysts.

The panther with the luxuriant coat took instantly to the luxurious lifestyle at the Schloss—where he dined on chinchillas and châteaubriand, lapped up saucers of Tokay and café au lait, and where his fur got a sandalwood soaping, his paws a pumice buffing, in his weekly bath.

manifest / manifold

☙ *Manifest* as an adjective means clearly apparent, obvious. *Manifold* means multiple, of many kinds, varied.

Manifest was Ilona's determination to outshop the Countess of Troo at the mall: she positively gloated with foolish purchases, and her American Express card emitted electric sparks.

Manifold revulsions await you as you round the Corner of Iniquity and enter the Hall of Bleeding Mirrors.

many

❧ Let us now enjoy a moment of silence to mourn the death of the word *many,* which has been replaced by *a lot of* and *lots of* in all public discourse.

Our numinous night visitor, with the mind of a Mediterranean miniature donkey, the eyes of a luxury class cat, had many mannerisms we took to without question, but his disappearances before daybreak left us restless, perplexed, and marooned.

much

❧ *Much* has gone the way of *many*—into oblivion—driven out by the same gadabouts: *lots of* and *a lot of.*

I owe you much gratitude: in what form do you wish me to offer it?
And where will you receive it?

Much clamor and clacking of castanets shattered the silence and rattled the duchess's sleep.

myself

 In presenting this overworked faux objective pronoun, Startling Glower retitled his program "Up Yourself's Eponym," with guests Strophe Dulac, Cedric Moltgang, and Vast Monthrock, Jr., tattooed and name-tagged MYSELF and using that pronoun where *me* belongs. Dulac overdid it altogether, replacing *I,* too, with *myself*—a less common and more serious error (and smacking of ingenue pretentiousness). In the Pronouns chapter of *The Deluxe Transitive Vampire,* the reflexive and intensive *-self* pronouns flex their muscles and flaunt their uses.

not:
If you wish to leave a message for Miranda or myself, please do so after the beep.

but:
If you wish to leave a message for Miranda or me, please do so after the beep.

not:
The party at The Zoological Gardens, a vegetarian restaurant, included Niles Galoof, Sasha Karlovsky, Kristine van Leeuwen Boomkamp, and myself.

but:
The party included Niles Galoof, Sasha Karlovsky, Kristine van Leeuwen Boomkamp, and me.

not:

"Hey, Fido, convey these slippers from me to himself!" barked one of the most disrespectful guests of the Schloss the panther had ever pondered mutilating with his claws.

but:

"Hey, Fido, convey these slippers from me to him!" barked one of the most disrespectful guests of the Schloss the panther had ever pondered mutilating with his claws.

not:

"My bestial entourage and myself shall go to the ball," said Cinderella to the sorceress who was tricking her out in see-through frippery, frangible footwear, and transportation by a team of plastered rodents.

but:

"My bestial entourage and I shall go to the ball," said Cinderella to the sorceress who was tricking her out in see-through frippery, frangible footwear, and transportation by a team of plastered rodents.

neither

❧ When *neither* is present in a sentence, the subject and the verb should agree, as should the noun and antecedent, and it's often singular that's called for.

Neither the cellist nor his cello gets through Ljubljana customs without brouhaha.

Neither of the baby dragons has swallowed the brooch of the Duchess of Malfatti.

Neither of the nannies was resistant to the baby vampire's tantrums.

Neither the dime store nor the alchemist's sells promises with its dangers.

❧ See also the Agreements chapter in *The Deluxe Transitive Vampire,* where these issues are giddily fondled.

none

🔆 Much confusion attaches to this lonely word, but that's partly because none of the rules (well, not many of them) are wearing chastity belts. When *none* really stands for *not one,* the verb is singular.

The three bridges have all been repeatedly assailed, but none has yet been carried away by either the river or the revolution.

🔆 When *none* is followed by a singular noun, it usually carries through with a singular verb.

None of the crème brûlée has burned my lips like the smack the bandit gave me.

This is, you know, the world premiere: none of *The Velveteen Rabble* has ever been performed in public by either the cast or the audience.

None of your silence speaks to me.

❧ A singular verb in the following and many other instances would be correct, but it is often disregarded or discarded in favor of the less pedantic-sounding plural verb.

None of the slanders were true, although Constanza was loath to deny them.

None of the girls in the harem were found wanting.

None of the enemy were roused by the blast.

And you really expect me to believe that none of you are to blame?

None of the audience were yawning or fidgeting yet; the costume changes were highly stimulating, and the opera was so far a hit.

None of the werewolves were at the drive-in watching *Truly, Madly, Deeply* on Walpurgisnacht.

 ❧ See also the Agreements chapter in *The Deluxe Transitive Vampire* for further illumination on *none*.

off

🐆 *Off* has no need of *of* to state its position. Usually *from* is also a needless syllable, except in the case of a merged verb such as "take off" for "depart," "become airborne": The plane took off from the tarmac.

not:
Get your mind off of me!

but:
"Get your mind off me, Torquil, and take your torso out of my teddy while you're at it!" said Jonquil, simulating a snarl.

not:
The prince is off of his rocker, and we should take him off of his mother's hands.

but:
The prince is off his rocker, and we should take him off his mother's hands.

The butler lifted the water wings off the panther's back and rubbed him down with a Turkish towel.

She took her clothes ruthlessly off the dresser, where she'd tossed them with circumspect abandon.

often

Like *frequently*, *often* has been ousted by an interloper running rampant through our quantifying and exaggerations. In many sentences, these words would be preferable, for sound, rhythm, alliteration, and variety. Preferable to *a lot of the time* or *lots of times.* That last sentence is a fragment; I hope it captured your attention. Not *got* your attention: another overworked word. *Much of the time* is another variation that might give *lot* a rest. Startling Glower still uses *oft,* while Aelfric Valinthrob antiquates the occasional clause with *oftnes,* just as he is wont to say *betimes* for *soon.* Every now and then even Fossilblast throws an *ofttimes* into the place of *oftentimes,* but Ampersand and Platgut both find all this posturing hyperliterary and archaic.

Clicking her tongue often,
she forgot the focus of her vengeance.

only

☙ Like *almost, even, hardly, nearly,* and *scarcely, only* should almost touch the word it modifies. In the first example, it's the teeth, and two more of them, at that, that are modified by *only*. This configuration is subtle but merits—and rewards—contemplation.

not:
The baby vampire only has two more teeth to grow and his mouth will be complete: then woe to a succession of nannies!

but:
The baby vampire has only two more teeth to grow and his mouth will be complete: then woe to a steady flow of susceptible, Type O nannies!

☙ In the following sentence, Jonquil is not really asking Torquil to only help her out of her teddy; she obviously has further requests she's about to press upon him. The second version is more fitting to this undressing and the ensuing frolics.

If you'd only help me out of this and then pull off my slippers very slowly and deliberately, we could wrestle in that bed of chamomile that grows like crazy when it's crushed.

If only you'd help me out of this and then pull off my slippers very slowly and deliberately, we could wrestle in that bed of chamomile that grows like crazy when it's crushed.

onto / on to

❧ *Onto,* a preposition in the following sentence, refers to a position, a placement of something; *on* is an adverb coupling with the preposition *to.* Drat Siltlow suggests that visualization may provide the key when you are trying to decide which to use.

She blew five kisses, stepped onto the plane, and clutched the St. Christopher at her throat.

She flew on to Amplochacha, where the symposium awaited her with its mazes and anfractuous turns of phrase.

We moved on to the next topic and kept our knuckles under control.

NOTE: *If we had moved onto the next topic, it would have had to have a physical presence among us, one we proceeded to stomp, step on, or, if it were full of air and our combined weights were massive, deflate.*

When we flipped a coin to see who'd strip first, it bounced from the table onto the floor and rolled leeringly (I refer to the portrait of our monarch on the silver zlotky) under the bed onto which we had meanwhile flung ourselves. This was long after he'd come on to me, on a barstool at Blotto Junction.

painful separations

❧ Zoë Platgut succinctly and smugly avers:
Misunderstandings, amusing or disastrous, can come along
with misplacements in the course of a sentence. Related
parts of a sentence want to stick together to make their
meaning felt. I myself have taken a vow not to sunder subject and predicate with brutality or nonchalance.

❧ Cram Fossilblast lays it on thick (modifying "it," not
"lays"): Why isolate a subject from its verb just when it's
ready for action? Why tease the star of your sentence so?
Should an adverb be skulking around the corner from the
verb it modifies? Does a phrase deserve to lie about so far
from its only reason for being there at all? And let's not for-
get clauses, those strung-out clodhoppers that can block
both entrance and exit or clot the very flow of meaning just
as it's found its way.

sundered:
You, waiting relentlessly for me at the corner, howled.

rejoined:
Waiting relentlessly for me at the corner, you howled.

At the corner where you awaited me relentlessly, you
howled.

separated:
Lada, in the silence enveloping this unexpected encounter with a mooncalf, loosened her vellum vest.

reunited:
In the silence enveloping this unexpected encounter with a mooncalf, Lada loosened her vellum vest.

subject and verb unbearably far apart:
I think that you, as a paragon of finesse and fashion and as an emblem of all that shines, should suppress those boxer shorts and see to those rebel tufts in your wings.

proximity restored:
I think that as a paragon of finesse and fashion and as an emblem of all that shines, you should suppress those boxer shorts and see to those rebel tufts in your wings.

I think that as a paragon of finesse and fashion, you should suppress those boxer shorts and see to those rebel tufts in your wings.

sundered:
I, placidly eating bonbons in my boudoir and caressing the panther with my slippered foot, left you with no succor to dulcify your doubts.

together:
Placidly eating bonbons in my boudoir and caressing the panther with my slippered foot, I left you with no succor to dulcify your doubts.

broken up:
Summon, after you've eyelined and talcum-powdered these hundred angels, me from my box at the opera.

back together:
After you've eyelined and talcum-powdered these hundred angels, summon me from my box at the opera.

apart:
Rumple, once you've received this message, the bedclothes in the master's chamber, then signal me stealthily from the North Tower.

together:
Once you've received this message, rumple the bedclothes in the master's chamber, then signal me stealthily from the North Tower.

  ⸮ Phrases, too, long to be placed near the words they modify.

far:
Let me know if you'll meet me in the quagmire by phone or telegram.

near:
Let me know by phone or telegram if you'll meet me in the quagmire.

amusingly positioned:
The damsel was nuzzling the
dazzled dragon in the Dior dress.

more likely, although less droll:
The damsel in the Dior dress was nuzzling the dazzled dragon.

    ⅞ And here, a participial phrase finds itself
attached to the wrong noun:

not:
Dancing lightly over the frosted cake Jesperanda beheld
the Bojangling rat tappers with their tails tucked into
their tights.

but:
Jesperanda beheld the Bojangling rat tappers dancing lightly
over the frosted cake, their tails tucked into their tights.

    ⅞ Clauses quite understandably clamor to
modify their words up close.

not:
She bartered her soul with the cloven-hoofed visitant
that she had just found.

but:
She bartered her soul, which she had just found, with the cloven-hoofed visitant.

not:
He whipped out the ace and flashed it at his captors that he had up his sleeve.

but:
He whipped out the ace that he had up his sleeve and flashed it at his captors.

not:
She flung her life beneath an oncoming train that she had decided to take.

but:
She flung her life, which she had decided to take, beneath an oncoming train.

᛭ Drat Siltlow says that even mere adjectives can creep away from the nouns they are meant to modify, and that these separations can sometimes escape our notice just as slyly as the greater ones we've already divulged.

misplaced adjective:
On the top shelf at the alchemist's they found a cache of sullied soubrettes' pinafores.

꙾ With the dirt where it belongs, since the soubrettes have immacu-late reputations:

On the top shelf at the alchemist's they found a cache of soubrettes' sullied pinafores.

misplaced:
A crumpled cow's horn was found beside a red glove on the floor of the powder room.

moved:
A cow's crumpled horn was found beside a red glove on the floor of the powder room.

꙾ This is not a very grave misplacement. Someone might get the idea that the cow had been abused or was suffering from rheumatoid arthritis, and hence was a bit pushed out of shape. But misunderstandings are unlikely here. And you could look at it this way: "cow's horn" taken all together is modified by "crumpled." In other words, these two words act as adjectives: "crumpled" + "cow's" modifying "horn."

꙾ When a modifier begins a sentence, the subject or noun it modifies should come immediately after it—and cer-tainly not be thrown out of modifying range by an inter-loper to which the adjective or phrase does not refer.

misplaced:
All ears and half-asleep, the rest of his tale of transgressions and tribulations was lost on her.

rearranged:
All ears and half-asleep, she missed the rest
of his tale of transgressions and tribulations.

another rearrangement, a more radical reconstruction:
The rest of his tale of transgressions and tribulations was lost
on her, since she was all ears but half-asleep.

misplaced:
Stalwart and seditious, the role of general factotum at the
Schloss was just her cup of schnapps.

rearranged:
Stalwart and seditious, she was cut out of the right stuff for
the role of general factotum at the Schloss.

pair

ᣟ· While the monumental dictionaries proclaim *pair* as a
plural of *pair* in informal exchanges, and the Oxford con-
tingent mentions its use after a numeral, Platgut reminds
her readers of a more rigorous approach, which I've applied
to the example sentences:
"The plural of *pair* is *pairs*. *Au pair* is a governess/comely
young servant on equal footing with the family of a house."

I have a pair each of breasts and wings, two pairs of legs, and a pair of tickets to *The Sorrows of Tristesse du Sanglot*. Would you care to accompany me?

Two pairs of red boots pattered down the hallway, and the puzzled panther pursued them with passionate and slinking stealth.

Naturally, the au pair, Katya, made a place for herself in the occasional orgy, and was soon breaking brioche with the Schloss's absent owner in his suite at Hotel Artaud.

parallel constructions

♪· Parallelism is a rhetorical trope if not a natural instinct that gives a sentence balance, rhythm, holds ideas in graspable shape. Here are several handfuls of such equilibrium in bestial and human forms (which, expressed in unparallel fashion, would say: "in bestial form and looking human"):

girls in puberty, cats in heat
fauns in pursuit, nymphs at ease
dragons of docile temperament, vampires of unslakeable thirst
rats of resplendent comeliness, ladies of slovenly déshabille
pythons that are fragile albinos, toads that are enchanted kings
spirits to uplift, despots to depose

♪· Parallel construction is especially effective for presenting ideas of equal value or emphasis—but not at the risk of sounding forced. To attack this at its simplest level, think of keeping adjectives paralleled by adjectives, nouns by nouns, infinitives by infinitives, subordinate clauses by subordinate clauses, and other such not too rigidly choreographed patterns.

He, she, and it all agreed on their common purpose at once. It was not iniquity, it was not treason, it was not even nonchalance.

♪· And now the awkward version:

It was not iniquity, there was no treason involved, and even nonchalance was far from their minds.

nonparallel:
Your new bustier is lascivious and an aphrodisiac and it scintillates. (adjective and noun and clause)

parallel:
Your new bustier is lascivious, aphrodisiacal, and scintillating. (three adjectives)

nonparallel:
The brigands had already begun sporting spats and to wear epaulettes of chinchilla fur. (mixing participial phrase and infinitive phrase)

parallel:
The brigands had already begun to sport spats and to wear epaulettes of chinchilla fur. (two infinitive phrases)

or:
The brigands had already begun sporting spats and wearing epaulettes of chinchilla fur. (two participial phrases)

nonparallel:
This infernal substance is terrifying to imagine, a pleasure to behold, and it is highly inflammable. (an adjective, a noun as appositive, and a clause)

parallel:
This infernal substance is a terror to imagine, a pleasure to behold, and a breeze to inflame. (three nouns as appositives)

nonparallel:

The symposium at Hotel Artaud will address these issues:

1. Care and how to feed the minotaur
2. Sustaining the maximum bewilderment for wanderers
3. What metaphors the labyrinth suggests for contemporary society

parallel:

The symposium at Hotel Artaud will address these issues:

1. Care and feeding of the minotaur
2. Strategies to sustain maximum bewilderment
3. Metaphors the labyrinth suggests for contemporary society

nonparallel:

Dragging the travelers from their troika was a pack of wolves with sheep's voices and they had bad manners and were roughly speaking and who kept their eyes on the jewels and were looking at the women's décolletage.

parallel:

Dragging the travelers from their troika was a pack of wolves with sheep's voices, bad manners, rough speech, and eyes fixed on the jewels and the women's décolletage.

Dragging the travelers from their troika was a pack of wolves speaking with sheep's voices, showing bad manners, using rough speech, and keeping their eyes on the jewels and the women's décolletage.

nonparallel:
The girls, after tearing into their packages and rolling around the floor among the wrappings, summed up their reactions by laughing hysterically and cross-eyed looks and a pantomime of effusive gratitude.

parallel:
The girls, after tearing into their packages and rolling around the floor among the ribbons and wrappings, summed up their reactions with hysterical laughter, cross-eyed looks, and a pantomime of effusive gratitude.

The girls, after tearing into their packages and rolling around the floor among the ribbons and paper, summed up their reactions by laughing hysterically, exchanging cross-eyed looks, and pantomiming effusive gratitude.

not:
I like him playing those pizzicato passages, how he rolls his
eyes, to watch him throwing his tails behind him as he attacks
the piano.

but:
I like his pizzicatoing, eye-rolling,
and throwing his tails behind him
as he attacks the piano.

I like to watch him play pizzicato passages, roll his eyes, and
throw his tails behind him as he attacks the piano.

not:
Let go of my pajamas, little darlin', and I wish you'd stop
crying and moaning.

but:
Let go of my pajamas, little darlin', and stop crying and
moaning.

or:
Let go of my pajamas, little darlin', and don't cry or moan.

or:
I wish you'd let go of my pajamas and stop crying and
moaning, little darlin'.

not:
The faun is farouche, with cloven hoofs, and behaves in a
sylvan fashion.

but:
The faun is farouche, cloven-hoofed, and sylvan.

or:
The cloven-hoofed faun is farouche and sylvan.

or:
The sylvan faun is cloven-hoofed and farouche.

not:
The black rats, so horrific in face and body, struck terror both awake and when sleeping.

but:
The black rats, so horrific in face and body, struck terror both awake and asleep.

not:
There were these long-necked cream-puffs fluffing about on the stage, vestigial wings protruding from their waistbands, and they batted at the azure air.

but:
There were these long-necked cream-puffs fluffing about on the stage, vestigial wings protruding from their waistbands, batting at the azure air.

About the stage fluffed long-necked cream puffs with vestigial wings protruding from their waistbands and batting at the azure air.

not:
Several bawdy, audacious fans were lying in lurk for him at the stage door, hoping to shake his hand and they wanted to get his autograph and maybe he'd tread on their toe shoes with his terpsichorean feet.

but:
Several bawdy, audacious fans were lying in lurk for him at the stage door, hoping to shake his hand, get his autograph, and have their toe shoes trampled by his terpsichorean feet.

not:
She has high cheekbones, her eyes appear apprehensive, and she is a good-looking babe.

but:
A good-looking babe, she has high cheekbones and apprehensive eyes.

or:
That babe has high cheekbones, apprehensive eyes, and good looks.

not:
There were no coins in her wallet, she didn't keep secrets in her drawers, and outsiders weren't to be seen in her face.

but:
She had no coins in her wallet, no secrets in her drawers, no outsiders in her face.

nonparallel:
Sonja Tweazle Scronx was a fine masseuse, a champ at Kung Fu, childlike in her spontaneity and could be very sweet like a child too, showed discretion about the au pair's secret *sorties,* outshone visiting musicians when she sang in her soprano voice and she was also a lutantist, which was a boon when she put the babies to sleep with lullabies at nap time and later when the youngsters were studying percussion and harp and took saxophone lessons.

parallel:
Sonja Tweazle Scronx was proficient in massage and Kung Fu, childlike in her spontaneity and sweetness, discreet about the au pair's secret *sorties,* and accomplished as a soprano and lutanist, the latter distinction initially a boon for the lullabies at nap time, and later for the youngsters' lessons on percussion, harp, and saxophone.

❧ When correlative conjunctions are at play, the elements about them should be parallel in form. This means minding where you place these little devils, too: *both . . . and; neither . . . nor; either . . . or; not only . . . but; whether . . . or.*

not:
Mog is not only celebrated as a concubine of potentates but also as a collector of rare lepidoptera.

but:
Mog is celebrated not only as a concubine of potentates but also as a collector of rare lepidoptera.

not:
We are fleeing both to Trajikistan and the Black Mountains for a respite from this insufferable giddiness.

but:
We are fleeing to both Trajikistan and the Black Mountains for a respite from this insufferable giddiness.

or:
We are fleeing both to Trajikistan and to the Black Mountains for a respite from this giddiness.

not:

She is unfathomable, with a head of strawberry blond hair, and has a deductive manner.

but:

She is deductive, strawberry blond, and unfathomable.

or:

She is an unfathomable, deductive strawberry blond.

or:

She is an unfathomable, strawberry blond deductress.

not:

He is cute, with a pinstriped soul, and has a dashing way about him.

but:

He is cute and dashing, with his pinstriped soul.

or:

He is cute and dashing, and his soul is pinstriped.

⁊· Startling Glower cites the first part of the following bit from Oliver Goldsmith's *She Stoops to Conquer* as a fine example of parallel construction, then throws in the rest as lagniappe:

If burning the footmen's shoes, frightening the maids, and worrying the kittens be humor, he has it. It was but yesterday he fastened my wig to the back of my chair, and when I went to make a bow, I popped my bald head in Mrs. Frizzle's face!

❧ A less parallel structure, Glower suggests, would read as follows, and here he adds an awkward shift in the second sentence, from active to passive voice:

If burning the footmen's shoes, then to bring on a fit of fear in the maids, and causing considerable worry among the kittens be humor, he is humorous indeed. It was but yesterday he fastened my wig to the back of my chair, and in my attempt to prostrate myself, my bald head was found to be popped in Mrs. Frizzle's face.

NOTE: *You'll find occasions when you want to jump the tracks and defy this convention, which is hardly an ironclad rule. This is one way to call attention, make a particular element stand out.*

She was born hairy and screeching, and has been a handful ever since.

❧ That break from adjectives to a noun is more effective, with a palpable image, than "and has been troublesome ever since." The reader can actually feel her ruckus and hairiness when invited to hold her in his hand.

I kiss you discreetly, but
with force, as we wind up this
chapter and subject.

precede / proceed

🦅 *Precede* means to come before something; *proceed* means
to get on with or move on to something, to go on with an
action.

The flight of the seraphim precedes the orgy of the velveteen
rabble, the exodus of the Norwegian rats, and the ravishment
of the lambkins of Dreadmore Valley.

The velveteen rabble proceeded with its deliberations,
lowering its raised hackles, mollifying its caustic phrases,
smoothing the furrows of its collective brow.

prefer

🦅 When *prefer* is followed by an infinitive, there's a way to
avoid having too many *to*'s ganging up on the sentence's
sound and sense: using *rather than*. In other instances, *prefer*
takes *over* or *to*.

She prefers tramps in tears to percussionists in tails.

I prefer *crème passionnelle* over chocolate decadence after that sacrificial lamb and pigweed with winking violets.

"I prefer to rumple your composure rather than to pay it false obeisance," explained the conductor to Duchess Ilona, who had designs on his harpist, a devil with too much gold in his mouth and a tail he dyed platinum blond when the orchestra was on tour in the provinces.

prophecy / prophesy

🜗 A *prophecy* is a foretelling, a prediction, and when more than one is coming at us, *prophecies* takes care of them. To utter a prophecy is to *prophesy,* rhyming with *eye,* while the noun rhymes with *see:* vision is often involved, making this mnemonic device apt.

Before the ravishment of Dreadmore Valley, prophecies proliferated of doom and debauchery, and self-flagellation was rife.

"I prophesy a visit of barbaric hordes with boundless savagery in their hearts, wrack and ruin on their minds," intoned the shepherd of the shorn and shaggy brethren who were quivering on the altar by the wine.

quizzical / inquisitive

"He has a quizzical mind."

🝰 Such a misuse could be cited as a supposed compliment in a letter of recommendation, misfiring and losing the inquisitive fellow the job, since the prospective employer, whose own vocabulary is more precise than this one's, would understand that the applicant is a mocking, teasing weirdo. *Quizzical* suggests puzzlement as well as eccentricity. *Inquisitive,* on the other hand (the right hand), does mean curious, mentally adventurous, full of questions, whether frivolous, prying, or profound.

The baby dragon gave the big bad panther a winsomely quizzical look that quite forfended the cat's malicious intentions.

"I have always admired your inquisitive mind, but take your inquisitions out of my dresser drawers," commanded Charmiane, who was packing for a weekend at the Schloss.

Mog had originally presented herself at court as a quizzical apparition in diaphanous draperies encircled by sluggish giant white moths. She followed this up with other fabled appearances that soon had the duke sending her shoe boxes of beribboned billets-doux and the title to his chalet on Lake Sandali.

rack / wrack

☙ A *rack* is a framework of various sorts, sometimes exceedingly painful. *To wrack* means to arrange on a rack, one that may involve torture. The noun *wrack* means ruin or destruction, and is rarely seen without its sidekick in the expression *wrack and ruin*. *Rack* is preferable to *wrack* as a verb, although in that capacity they mean much the same thing. Preferable in usage, that is; racking is an activity you are wise to shun. Natty Ampersand tried it before fashioning such a supple noose.

The chef left some brownies made of volcanic ash, tar, and burnt sugar on the cookie rack, where they were discovered by one of the little dragons, who was snorting about for a *friandise*.

This Schloss has been visited by wrack and ruin repeatedly in its past, but these days it's visited mostly by misbehavior and mirth—at least until those banditti bungled their midnight call.

rarely

🎵 *Rarely ever* is redundant, but *rarely if ever* are the mots justes every now and then. *Seldom* partakes of the same pattern.

"Rarely if ever has such a placid scene been described in literature," wrote critic Cedric Moltgang of Chapter Twelve, where the heroine (protagonist would be much too frisky a word) of *Torpor in the Swing* studies her tube of Humeur Noire lipstick and fails to commence her toilette.

rather than

🎵 Parallel construction is a noble aim when *rather than* is in the midst of things. *More* should not be included in such instances: if you want to use it, leave *rather than* out of the picture altogether.

not:
He tried humiliating rather than to seduce me.

but:
He tried humiliating rather than seducing me.

not:
She aimed more at pleasing herself rather than at cajoling and caressing the crowd.

but:
She aimed more at pleasing herself than at cajoling and caressing the crowd.

ravage / ravish

🎗 *Ravish* means to carry away with emotion in its mildest sense, to rape or abduct in its roughest. *To ravage* is to devastate, to wreak horrific destruction.

Having ravaged numerous sordid and picturesque, compressed and adorable, fetid and historic *quartiers,* Baron Haussmann rolled out his *grands boulevards,* making way for the sauntering *mode de vie* of the *flâneur,* grisette, and dandy.

"I was merely jesting when I said 'Pardon my shabby getup and ravish me again,' " said Ilona. "You know perfectly well I don't like having my feathers ruffled."

He ravished her bosom, her midriff, her governess, while the other banditti set fire to her floor plans, but in shuffled the sleepwalking butler, the panther at his heels, and the miscreants took to *their* heels, spattering blood in frenzied patterns as they careened through the woods, for none had escaped the wrath of the big black cat, the Schloss's scourge and security system.

reason

❧ *Reason* is followed by *that* or *why,* not *because,* whether you are offering excuses or subtleties of logic.

The reason Cinderella arrived late at the ball was that the rats drawing her glass-bottomed coach had been guzzling champagne from her electric footbath.

The reason the rats got plastered is that they didn't often come across a jeroboam of Veuve Clicquot, and Cinderella was having trouble with her stockings and strapless bra.

not:
The reason I'm spreading slanders about you is because you've put a curse on my curvaceous niece.

but:
The reason I'm relenting is that my perfidious rumors have brought you to your knees.

He offered no reason, plausible or far-fetched, why he wanted to borrow my lorgnette, angora sweater, and stiletto heels.

The reason we won't be home for your visit is that we'll be bugging your pleasure dome and your yacht the *Scarlatina.*

NOTE: *In this last sentence, there is no comma after* yacht *because the* Scarlatina *is but one of several yachts belonging to this ostentatious and* *dysfunctional family, too much explosive psyche for one mere vessel to contain. If they had only one yacht, its name would be supplementary information and therefore set off by a comma.*

"Won't you tell me the reason why you're confiscating my innocuous book?" asked Laurinda of the bibliophobic border guard.

regarded

᠅ *Being* does not follow *regarded as:* jump right ahead with the statement's completion.

not:
She is regarded as being the niftiest nymph in the glade by all the fauns in the locker room.

but:
She is regarded as the niftiest nymph in the glade by all the fauns in the locker room.

not:
She is regarded as being the sauciest sorceress that ever licked flames in all Trajikistan.

but:
She is regarded
as the sauciest
sorceress that ever licked flames in all Trajikistan.

regardless

> 🔸 Disregard *irregardless.*

Regardless of what you think of me, I'll always be Troo to you, said the discomposed Countess, who sincerely wanted to part friends without plastering her heart on his undershirt.

reluctant / reticent

> 🔸 Both words denote unwillingness—*reluctant,* to act; *reticent,* to speak.

Laurinda was reluctant to look the border guard in the eyes, but she knew that if she allowed her hesitation to show, she might well spend her honeymoon in a dungeon and savage her uncle Nimbo's chances with several collusions in Mitteleuropa.

Charmiane, to protect her secret drawer, faked reticence about many unrelated subjects that had no claim on her soul, and thus it was impossible to conduct the most innocent conversation without her rapid evasions and divagations, consultations of dictionaries and atlases, rattlings of her reticule, tappings on her laptop, cigarettes lit at the wrong end, and intercontinental faxes.

review / revue

꙳ A *review* is a critical consideration or report of something (art exhibit, movie, book, fashion show). A *revue* might be reviewed, in the tabloid or other press: it's a type of light, amusing theater show.

His scathing review of *The Moon Has Two Faces* included the reflections of two astrophysicists known for their panache and cosmic epigrams, and a profile shot of the author swimming in two directions.

The revue that followed this pompous oration featured a siren in mouse trappings doing *Thus Spake Zarathustra* as an interplanetary cellular phone call about an American Express bill for three nights at The Last Judgment Pinball Machine Motel.

rifle / riffle

꙾ *Rifle* is a transitive verb meaning to ransack and rob, to plunder or strip bare, to steal or take away.

The brutes rifled the linen closet and abducted my smutty books cached beneath the flannel sheets.

꙾ *Riffle* can be either a transitive or intransitive verb meaning to turn hastily, flutter, and shift: to riffle a stack of letters, to riffle through a book.

"Some fetishistic vandal's been riffling through my underwear!" bellowed Charmiane, merely feigning indignation and apprehension, since her secret drawer remained inviolate and unbesmirched.

I riffled *The Pastel Maniac* hastily and tucked the incriminating documents into the removable back of my massive hairbrush as we approached the border and anticipated the thorough search already fluttering the hands of the officials.

scarcely

꙾ Leave out *not* or its contraction when using *scarcely,* which is already negative.

not:
I couldn't scarcely remember his name, I was so astonished to find him stretched out in suspicious splendor across my mosaic doorstep.

but:

I could scarcely remember his name, I was so astonished
to find him stretched out in suspicious splendor across
my mosaic doorstep.

NOTE: *You will come to a caution about* so. *The above sentence isn't
really a violation of Zoë's mild injunction, since the sentence, rearranged, would read: I was so astonished to find him on my doorstep
(that) I could scarcely remember his name.*

꙳ It is easy to misplace *scarcely* and muddle your meaning.
Give the sentence a good look and be sure *scarcely* is near the
word it modifies, to avoid a painful separation.

not:

We scarcely were aware of the menace gliding through the
corridor.

but:

We were scarcely aware of the menace gliding through the
corridor.

🔸 *Scarcely,* like those other adverbs we've nuzzled (*barely, hardly*), needs no *not* to convey its meaning.

not:
I didn't scarcely get a look at his mug before I too was blindfolded.

but:
I scarcely got a look at his mug before I too was blindfolded.

second hand / secondhand

🔸 *Second hand* is a noun, the kind to be found in action on the face of a watch or clock. *Secondhand* is used as either an adjective or an adverb.

The second hand had lost its bearings and was shuttling frantically between the 5 and the 8, while the minute hand serenely continued its stately, cosmic sweep.

I bought this amphora secondhand off an antiquarian from Azuriko.

Secondhand aperçus meet with frosty silence, open scoffing, or lofty disdain at Cedric Moltgang's table. It's best to compose several mouthfuls of epigrams in advance to see you safely through the postprandial babble.

shall / will

⨎ Zoë Platgut revised her thinking on *shall/will,* bringing her future up to date, after a French coiffeur had had his way with her hair and given her sartorial advice. She long ago dropped the archaic-sounding *shan't* and other oddities inflicted on her in tyrannical boarding schools. There and then, *shall* was used for first person, *will* for second and third person to express simple futurity. Furthermore, the order was reversed to express determination (to bring in willfulness, even with *shall*). Now *shall* is used less frequently, and when it is, it conveys more decorum, formality and/or determination—another tone entirely. Post-Modernist Drat Siltlow points out the prevalence of contractions, which sidestep these choices by folding in the first letters of each word:

We'll see about these outrageous eyebrows after
we've shaved your neck and waxed your legs.

You'll regret it if you make a botch of it—and
don't you touch my wings!

⨎ Our Restoration fop quotes Congreve to show *shall* in conjugal action:

"I shall by degrees dwindle into a wife."

𝄐 Platgut, speaking for the conservatives, crisply blares: "*So* is not an adverb meaning *very very, very much, extremely, excessively,* although it is so often commandeered to mime this message that there will soon be few who remember its intended purposes. When used with an adjective, it occurs in constructions like the one we just left: *so often . . . that.* The *so* announces an upshot and feels abused when nothing happens, that is, follows." Platgut makes her point most cruelly by citing the final sentence of *Out of the Loud Hound of Darkness:*

She was so touched by his condolences that she murdered the rest of her relatives.

𝄐 And now for some gentler examples:

Constanza was so obsessed with Mozart that she wore her hair as he did.

NOTE: *In the above example,* as *is called for, not* like. *See* like/as.

𝄐 If I'd desperately wanted to use *like,* I'd rewrite the sentence:

Constanza was so obsessed with Mozart that she wore her hair like his.

𝄐 *That* is not always necessary. It can be hidden, implied:

One of the bandits was so craven he hid beneath Duchess Ilona's dresser when he heard the panther's paws padding past the open door.

Although he generally disdained floral arrangements, Mucho Trabajo was so hungry that he nipped at his mistress's corsage as she turned to address the duchess.

   Ч *So* also shows great promiscuity in contexts where it means *for that reason,* and is strung along in the fashion this sad story displays.

He stood me up so I got miffed so I came on to his best friend, so he got mad and retaliated by catnapping my ocelot, only I didn't find that out till I'd put an ad in *The Weekly Swinger* and received fifty calls, all false leads, so I wound up changing my phone number.

   Ч A more finely wrought version, because more varied, the elements looped together in a more expressive structure without losing the colloquial flavor of the language:

Because he stood me up and I got miffed, I came on to his best friend, in retaliation for which he catnapped my ocelot. I didn't find out, however, till I'd placed an ad in *The Weekly Swinger* and received fifty calls, all false leads, which drove me to change my phone number.

so as

☞ *So as* often injects redundancy into a sentence with an infinitive. It's unnecessary; Platgut calls it a nuisance.

not:

He hijacked her Bugatti and abducted her ocelot so as to avenge her dalliance. The ransom he demanded was a torrid night of love, with the ocelot caterwauling in the background.

but:

He hijacked her Bugatti and abducted her ocelot to avenge her dalliance. The ransom he demanded was a torrid night of love, with the ocelot caterwauling in the background.

split infinitives

☞ Vargas Scronx demonstrates this sometime faux pas before donning his Medieval equipage and becoming more complicated: "To split an infinitive, all you have *to* unconsciously or consciously *do* is *to* as I am doing here *string* several words between the parts of the infinitive form, between the *to* and the rest of the action or passion or repose or motion. This interruption in the verb form rarely obscures the meaning, loses the reader, or creates the slapstick mental pictures that dangling modifiers and other awkward separations and misplacements evoke for our amusement if not confusion."

❧ Aelfric Valinthrob indulges in a digression with an archaic verb before discussing aesthetics:

"A word that comes to mind for this verb form is the double-meaning *cleave:* in wedding vows and declarations of love, 'I cleave to you' comes close to meaning 'I'm stuck on you'—or at least 'I'm holding on tight, even swearing fidelity.' Cleaving, however, can also mean severing, splitting apart. The infinitive, destined to enact both connotations, still means just what it is: mentally, we'll pull it together when it's disporting about a sentence. Rarely will a *to* be so alienated from the verb, as in the opening sentences of this section, that they'll seem unacquainted. In one's writing, sometimes adverbs intervene because one *wants* the verb and its modifier to rub each other the wrong way, or in some way that startles them both into a different meaning through a difficult alliance."

split:
He begged her *to* indecently *think* of him.

together:
He begged her *to think* of him indecently.

together:
He begged her *to think* indecently of him.

split:
She asked him *to* dexterously *manipulate* her.

together:
She asked him *to manipulate* her dexterously.

> ☞ In both the above instances, the sentence reads better with the break repaired. Zoë, no doubt dreaming of one of those afternoons in an Emirate armchair, intrudes with a variation that she claims makes more blatant her wishes by inserting the adverb insinuatingly in the infinitive's midst:

She invited him to ambidextrously arouse her.

split:
It's best to a week in advance compose several bons mots to safely see you through the postprandial bosh and babble.

repaired:
It's best to compose several bons mots a week in advance to see you safely through the postprandial bosh and babble.

old-fashioned repair, sounding awkward:
It's best to compose several bons mots a week in advance safely to see you through the postprandial bosh and babble.

infinitive split:

He groped for some approximate translation of a French idiom and came up with "to securely be sewn into a cloud."

infinitive sewn back together:
He groped for some approximate translation of a French idiom and came up with "to be securely sewn into a cloud."

NOTE: *In this story of the idiom, the split version is especially inappropriate as "sewn" is the key word and image (of this compound verb) and should stick close to the adverb "securely."*

⚡ In the following, I have my reasons for preferring the infinitive cut open to make way for intimations.

The vampire powdered his nose and cheeks *to* coyly *camouflage* his astoundingly radiant good looks.

⚡ I want to emphasize his intentions, letting the reader's eye and mind fix on "coyly," and look for a moment into his soul. He has his ways, this one, of approaching his victims or going to parties; he doesn't pounce and grab right off. There's a *sound* reason for this also: two adverbs ending in *-ly* too close together make this a less fetching sentence. I don't want to rewrite the sentence to remove an adverb, because I like the way these two play against each other: "coy" is practically contradicted by "astoundingly radiant," so we see his duplicity at work.

⋟ Infinitives appear in questions such as "To be or not to be?" "To lower my hemline or to let down my hair with farouche panache?" and "To go to the ball in necromantic trappings or not to go at all?" If Shakespeare had split infinitives on their way out of his melancholy Dane's mouth, the soliloquy would begin, "To be or to not be?" And the ingenue or octogenarian adventuress would be wondering, "To lower my hemline or to with farouche panache let down my hair?" while Cinderella would be asking her reflection, "To go to the ball in necromantic trappings or to not go at all?"

squinting modifiers

⋟ A squinting modifier is one placed between two words so that it could be construed to modify either word. It's been rumored that Startling started to glower when on the look for these. Often, a discreetly positioned *that* can clear up the ambiguity. Otherwise, rechoreograph parts of the sentence so the right things are touching.

squinting:
She said yesterday she lost her ocelot.

clear:
Yesterday she said she lost her ocelot.
She said she lost her ocelot yesterday.

squinting:
The faun announced this morning he hurt his hoof.

clear:
This morning the faun announced he hurt his hoof.
The faun announced he hurt his hoof this morning.
The faun announced that he hurt his hoof this morning.

squinting:
The generalissimo announced last week some mercurial mercenaries and brigands with fans had joined the troops without his authorization.

clear:
The generalissimo announced that last week some mercurial mercenaries and brigands with fans had joined the troops without his authorization.

Last week the generalissimo announced that some mercurial mercenaries and brigands with fans had joined the troops without his authorization.

squinting:
He says tonight he'll be right up my alley.

clear:
He says he'll be right up my alley tonight, but I'll be out on the avenida selling potions in my pram.

He says he'll be right up my alley tonight, but I'll be out selling potions in my pram on the avenida.

Tonight he says he'll be right up my alley, but he could change his tune tomorrow when he finds out what I'm trafficking when he's out of town.

⅄ Sometimes it is necessary to split a compound verb in order to escape this confusion, as we see with the Doppel- gänger and "was grimacing," as well as with the wearer of seraphic slippers who ran or flew in from an earlier entry.

squinting:
The Doppelgänger who was grimacing ruthlessly stalked his other half.

clear:
The Doppelgänger who was ruthlessly grimacing stalked his other half.

clear:
The Doppelgänger who was grimacing stalked his other half ruthlessly.

squinting:
She even had bought a silver negligee with wings sprouting out of the shoulders, and winged slippers to match.

clear:
She had even bought a silver negligee with wings sprouting out of the shoulders, and winged slippers to match.

straight-laced / strait-laced

꙳ Although dictionaries may offer these two words as twins in meaning, and some remove the hyphen, several usage-mongers (my own snored through the interrogation) make the following distinction, maintaining that *strait* has to do with constriction, as in *straitjacket, straight* with morals, conventionality, by extension meaning heterosexual.

꙳ Here's the distinction at work, all laced up with somewhere to go: *Straight-laced* is applied to those severe in behavior or morality; *strait-laced* conveys the notion of confinement, such as corsets and other gothic underwear inflict on their occupants.

Straight-laced behavior was banned for three weeks every four months throughout Louvelandia under the reign of Placido V. Residents who preferred to cling to their inhibitions were bussed and ferryboated (on the house: the royal household, that is) into Blegue, where they were observed with chagrined incomprehension by anthropologists, criminologists, and the duchess's *corps d'esprits.*

Slinking into the strait-laced bodice and stranglehold waistband was a cinch for the lovely lamia: she had been slithering from the day she was born, and was equally adept at ingress and egress, embraces, fissures, closets, clothing, and parentheses.

subjects / nouns
shifts in person

𝄞 A noun as subject wants to maintain its identity from the beginning to the end of its moment in a sentence. Zoë Platgut suggests in no uncertain terms that a writer can see to this by not shifting around person and number of the same noun in different elements of the sentence in which the noun is imperiled (Valinthrob says "impaled").

shifty:
When you are crazy in love, one is fearful of one's own faults.

faithful:
When you are crazy in love, you are fearful of your own faults.

When one is crazy in love, one might be oblivious to one's own faults.

shifty:
When one becomes a streetwalker, you don't write home very much.

faithful:
When you become a streetwalker, you don't write home very much.

When one becomes a streetwalker, one doesn't write home very much.

not:
You can catch the blues without meaning to when you flood one's rooms with their raucous, plangent wails.

but:
You can catch the blues without meaning to when you flood your carefree chambers with their raucous, plangent wails.

NOTE: *When* one *possesses, the possession is not* his *or* hers: *it's* one's.

One must have one's suspenders on tight to bounce along the boulevard as a full-fledged, convincing sprite.

    ♪ Cram Fossilblast, with Malvolio on his mind, sets him afoot in a city of Shakespeare's time or ours.

not:
One must step mincingly over the flooded gutter if one is to keep his kneecaps dry and yellow garters clean.

but:
One must step mincingly over the flooded
gutters if one is to keep one's kneecaps dry and
one's yellow garters clean.

shifts in number

not:
If a faun becomes thirsty, they find a stream.

but:
If a faun becomes thirsty, he finds a stream.

or:
If fauns become thirsty, they find a stream.

not:
After a faun takes his nap, they lick their hoofs and then rub
their eyes.

but:
After a faun takes his nap, he licks his hoofs and then rubs his
eyes.

or:
After fauns take their naps, they lick their hoofs and then rub
their eyes.

not:

When a faun falls in love, they are mocked without mercy by his friends.

but:

When a faun falls in love, he is mocked without mercy by his friends.

not:

If a dragon senses danger, they pretend they're fast asleep and fiercely dreaming.

but:

If a dragon senses danger, it pretends it's fast asleep and fiercely dreaming.

If dragons sense danger, they pretend they're fast asleep and fiercely dreaming.

subjects /  nouns with appositives

⁊ Appositives are applauded and paraded in *The Deluxe Transitive Vampire* and comma'd in *The New Well-Tempered Sentence,* but the warning about misplacements they can trip off is flash-book material. When a sentence begins with an appositive, the subject should come quickly, with no other substantives intervening and falsely claiming kinship. Verbose appositives can be so vivid and captivating that the subject might be forgotten before it's been announced: noun or pronoun, proper or improper, a rose, a tiger, a fiend. In the first example, Amaranthia is the noun in apposition to the loftily described factotum, so *they* should buzz off altogether or get rewritten into another position. I've fleshed and furred them out in my second version.

misplaced:
A factotum of imponderable eyes and discretion, they saddled Amaranthia with full responsibility for keeping the Schloss up to snuff.

rearranged:
A factotum of great charm and sang-froid, Amaranthia was saddled with full responsibility for keeping the Schloss up to snuff, once the butler, panther, absent owner, and nanny had assessed her capacities.

misplaced:
A rare and notorious river girlbeast, the paparazzi were just seconds too late as Isolde flourished her shiny tail at them and disappeared into the darkling waters, with nothing but a lusty splash, then an arabesque of ripples to greet the flash of their cameras.

rearranged:
The paparazzi were just seconds too late as Isolde, a rare and notorious river girlbeast, flourished her shiny tail at them and disappeared into the darkling waters, with nothing but a lusty splash, then an arabesque of ripples to greet the flash of their cameras.

misplaced:
Photojournalist, swashbuckler, brothel creeper, art historian, *Menace in Venice* is Dash Siebenthrall's first Adriatic Carnivalesque psychological thriller.

rearranged:
Menace in Venice is the first Adriatic Carnivalesque psychological thriller by Dash Siebenthrall, the photojournalist, swashbuckler, brothel creeper, and art historian.

Photojournalist, swashbuckler, brothel creeper, art historian, Dash Siebenthrall is making his literary debut with *Menace in Venice,* an Adriatic Carnivalesque psychological thriller.

taunt / tout

꙳ *Taunt* is to tease in a particularly torturous or tantalizing or provocative way. *Tout* means to brag about, sing the praises of, and does not take a preposition to do so.

Since everything depended on a fully considered answer, her eyes scanned the heavens for inspiration, an augury, an angel with a mot juste on his lips and a taunting wink, a suggestive flutter of his wings.

Touting the topography as one of the most morose on the dark side of Mitteleuropa, the Trajikistan tourist bureau brought out a brochure with shots of its black crystal crags and its caverns of bats and lost pedestrian echoes. Inside, too, the traveler's fingers fumbled upon a miniature relief map of the country's brooding mountains.

that

🎵 Vargas Scronx writes: "*That* is often accompanied by a Doppelgänger, an entirely useless companion." In a rare display of fervid bravura, Platgut warns against straying with *that* into the realm of superfluity, where many a lollygagging miscreant has met his epistemological doom.

not:
We know that, although he is patting her midriff, *that* things will go no further for quite some time.

but:
We know that, although he is patting her midriff, things will go no further for quite some time.

not:
They supposed that, even if they melted down all the calendars and smashed all the clocks, *that* one minute would daftly follow another until some final cure were found for the ravaging malady of time.

but:
They supposed that, even if they melted down all the calendars and smashed all the clocks, one minute would daftly follow another until some final cure were found for the ravaging malady of time.

that / which

❧ *That* and *which* refer to places, animals, and objects (stuffed animals, lost keys, maps of the heavens, mauled and tattered dictionaries, portfolios, bonbons, events such as cataclysms and trysts). *That* is used to introduce essential clauses, while *which* is used to introduce nonessential clauses, ones not necessary to identify the subject or object, but which add extra information, an afterthought, a bit of embroidery or imbroglio. In the first sentence the clause is nonessential because the boots are already identified as being hers and red. Unless she has a closet full of red boots of various designs and origins, and the identity of this pair must be refined through the anecdote about the Hungarian corpse, then a comma follows "boots" and *which* kicks off the anecdote.

Her red boots, which she'd bought from a fawning undertaker who'd removed them from the comely corpse of a Hungarian dancer, pinched her toes and gave out vicious squeaks.

The funeral parlor that was the venue of this sordid exchange had always enjoyed a spotless reputation.

The question, which had to be phrased delicately, concerned a cello case and its contents.

In her rickety garret, which was crawling with rats, she mapped out her departure for Trajikistan.

NOTE: *Here,* which *is the word we want because we already know that it's* her *garret, and that's plenty of restriction for one garret. The rats, however much they add to the ambiance, are not necessary to identify the venue of her strategizing.*

In a rickety garret that was crawling with rats she conjured alternative scenarios.

NOTE: *That* is conjured *here as well to further specify this anonymous garret.*

That bewildered bedroom of baby dragons, which was left on the doorstep of the Schloss, is the fault of Valinthrob.

NOTE: *As the bedroom is identified as* that *one,* and a bewildered, an-*thropomorphized one to boot, with feelings that is (its walls must have ears, and if so, eyes, which weep for the infants' plight),* which *is what is called for.*

The tempests that are in our teapots are advancing toward the platter of cakes.

Trinculo's own personal tempest, which is under wraps, won't help me drown my sorrows.

The baby dragon that went scouting for a nanny came back disheartened and distraught.

NOTE: *This brave and desperate soul needs further distinguishing from his fellows: he's the one that "went scouting," not the others that remained at this strange new place and wondered what would become of them.*

NOTE: *Ever a fiend for hallucinogenic details, Drat Siltlow zeroes in on these frightening exceptions to the usual that / which, essential / nonessential distinctions.*

❖ *Which* is preferable to *that* when two or more parallel essential clauses are acting up in the same sentence or when the essential clause begins with an expression such as *this . . . which, that . . . which, these . . . which, those . . . which.*

Loona is sending out post cards which will arouse your wanderlust and send you packing and which will cause you to drop everything at once but your suitcase and panoply of false mustaches and fake passports.

That is one place which you must avoid if you value your life—or your wife.

That is one place you must avoid if you value your life—or your wife.

🎵 Another instance for choosing *which* over *that* to introduce an essential clause is when *that* has just been used in the same sentence, and you wish to avoid repetition. "This," says Drat, "is an aesthetic choice, one of those decisions which should be made *à l'improviste.*"

That's one mermaid who hasn't succumbed to the swashbuckling, bisexual charms of the second mate, Ziggie Spurthrast. She has a *je ne sais quoi* about her, though, that sticks to your memory like Spanish flypaper and which evokes memories of a girl's first kiss or a tomboy's tumble from a treetop.

that / who

𝄐 Natty Ampersand harangued an audience of "Up Your Eponym" on this issue, and also wrote the following in a column before disappearing himself:

𝄐 "Where, oh where, has *who* gone? *That* has kicked *who* out of its rightful place, beside any person being discussed, and is dehumanizing us all very fast. Use *who* for humans and also for animals with names; animals without names must suffer the indignity of taking a *that* or a *which,* depending on how essential or nonessential the clause. Although *that* is acceptable for persons, it's being overworked."

The odious task fell to his faithful retainer, Capriccio, who had served him through the Cashmere Crisis and the case of the lapsed credenza.

Rafael Todos los Muertos, who carried his wing in a sling after that ruckus at the saloon, put out a contract on Dante Kaputo, who was pursuing Dusty Saxon through the canyons of Azuriko.

The droshky bore mufflered emissaries, who all wore side whiskers, cravats with the Czarina's insignia, and the most fetching, fatigued little frowns.

Laurinda sent a coded telegram to her uncle Nimbo, who was at the top of the hit list, and had investments in Bosoxian pizza parlors, what's more.

not:
Well, I think you have to watch your step with someone that's flashing such flagrant signals while buying you drinks and splashing your blouse with whiskey.

but:
Well, I think you have to watch your step with someone who's flashing such flagrant signals while buying you drinks and splashing your blouse with whiskey.

not:
And thanks to all you folks out there that make it possible for us to keep our studio cranking out this schlock.

but:
And thanks to all you folks out there who make it possible for us to keep our studio cranking out this schlock.

not:
There was this girl that had one of those Cheshire cat grins and a pack of rats in her reticule.

but:
There was this girl who had one of those Cheshire cat grins and a pack of rats in her reticule.

not:
Mucho Trabajo is the wistful donkey that's placed that come-on in the personals.

but:
Mucho Trabajo is the wistful donkey who's placed that come-on in the personals.

The mastodon that had had his way with her petits fours trained his tusks on her *crème passionnelle*.

Allegro non Troppo, the mastodon who had had his way with her petit fours, trained his tusks on her *crème passionnelle*.

The faun, who was positively gleaming with indolence, watched Narcissus with disbelief.

> ❧ *That* is used when a class or type of person is involved.

Are you the sort of girl that entertains her diary with whopping lies and treats strangers to true confessions?

Are you the sort of faun that slinks past glades and eavesdrops while nymphs discuss their conquests and wax their legs?

'til / till / until

> ❧ These all mean the same thing. *'Til* is tending toward obsolescence, and *'till* is a total faux pas.

I'll wait by the severed black oak 'til the tower rocks with a bloodcurdling yell or the butler emerges from the pergola to take the panther for his evening stroll.

Orgies at the Schloss generally go on until the last bacchant or bacchante drops.

Yours till the tides rebuff the moon, till the
dawn brings a gang of stars,
                              Loona

tortuous / torturous

❧ *Tortuous* means winding, crooked, full of twists and turns: anfractuous! *Torturous* means full of or causing pain, torture, torment.

The least tortuous of the labyrinths discussed at the symposium—the one in the national library of Blegue— is full of pools of light and pleasant distractions (books) besides an occasional muffled scream.

Racking my brain is child's play compared to the torturous interrogation I was subjected to at the border of Blegue. After that, they rifled my luggage and confiscated my hookah, knickers, camera obscura, and my autographed copy of *The Pastel Maniac*.

toward / towards

❧ Both words are correct. *Toward* is more frequently used, but you might occasionally wish to slide into the rest of a sentence with that final *s* to create a more mellifluous or alliterative sound.

Coming towards them through the darkness was a mass of faceless, cloakless malevolence that was immanent in the grove of quaking aspens at that time every year.

Drive toward the cathedral till you come to the statue of Incognito V on his bicycle, then veer sharply to the right— and head toward Café Sans-Culottes et Compagnie, where I shall await you with the Plume dossier.

try to / try and

❧ *Try and* is not the expression; *try to* is.

not:
Try and keep your socks on, Bottie, and compose your collar and toupee.

but:
Try to keep your socks on, Bottie, and compose your collar and toupee.

unconscious / unconscionable

☞ *Unconscious* is not conscious: knocked out, dead to the world, asleep. *Unconscionable* relates to deeds, ones that one's conscience would find difficult to accept, forgive—insupportable to the conscience.

The sandman, sure of Miranda's unconscious condition and his powers of somnolent seduction, was less successful than he assumed as he tiptoed from her bedside: she was merely faking sleep before returning to *The Haunted Reticule* and its glittering dénouement.

Stealing the sequined reticule with its rich endowments (traveler's checks, emeralds, seven wedding rings, a souvenir program signed by Constanza Zermatress) would have been an unconscionable act for a guttersnipe, a delectable coup for a dandified thief.

unique

❧ *Unique,* meaning one of a kind, does not leave itself open to comparisons such as *very unique, more unique, most unique.*

The lamia, unique among the lissome beauties showing off their legs and dubious talents, was of supernatural and infernal origin.

The reign of Incognito VI was unique in three ways: it collected no taxes, it showered favors on peasants, and it kept its king in a shack.

 ## upward

❧ *Upward* is correct; *upwards* is slightly infra dig, although it does blaze a place for itself in the expression "upwards of," meaning "more than."

There seemed to be only one way to go in the tower—upward—and this impression was reinforced by how vigorously he was shoving me up the stairs.

Onward and upward we believed we were going, but at what a ridiculous angle!

That ridiculous angel who harps on guitars commands upwards of five thousand zlotky per concertina—her name for a little concert.

verbs

❧ There are several consistencies to keep in mind as you juggle and impale your verbs so that you don't shift from one voice, tense, or mood to another while careening through a sentence.

shifts in tense

not:
She lumbered across the verandah and proceeds to lament.

but:
She lumbered across the verandah and proceeded to lament.

not:
She enters from the left and began unraveling the scholar's muffler.

but:
She entered from the left and began unraveling the scholar's muffler.

or:
She enters from the left and begins unraveling the scholar's muffler.

not:
This story recounts the adventures of a hypochondriac who
has been plagued by an aberrant kneecap and had tried several
miracle cures and then takes matters into his own hands and
drowned himself, lured by the anodyne arias of sirens.

but:
This story recounts the adventures of a hypochondriac who
has been plagued by an aberrant kneecap and has tried several
miracle cures and then takes matters into his own hands and
drowns himself, lured by the anodyne arias of sirens.

not:
The Champion of Valenciennes is a proletarian drama about a
scrap of lace, and a mere slip of a girl who liberates a
basement of child laborers and left a cache of white collars
undone.

but:
The Champion of Valenciennes is a proletarian drama about a
scrap of lace, and a mere slip of a girl who liberates a
basement of child laborers and leaves a cache of white collars
undone.

not:
She winds up her alarming clock and lay down in green
pastures, where last night's implacable sheep have knocked
over the fences and were nibbling away at her floor plans.

but:
She winds up her alarming clock and lies down in green
pastures, where last night's implacable sheep have knocked
over the fences and are nibbling away at her floor plans.

not:
He let out a wild shrill hiccup, yelps, "Yahoo!" and had
a go at the Doberman.

but:
He lets out a wild shrill hiccup, yelps, "Yahoo!" and has
a go at the Doberman.

or:
He let out a wild shrill hiccup, yelped, "Yahoo!" and had a go
at the Doberman.

shifts in voice

ᚅ· Before we move on to the shifts within sentences, here
are a few examples of active and passive voice in action and
passivity.

passive:
The cat's paw was torn on an avenging angel's wing.

active:
The cat tore its paw on an avenging angel's wing.

active:
Trotting into the piano room, Sir Tazzlemunk torched the harping angel.

passive:
The harping angel was torched by Sir Tazzlemunk as he trotted into the piano room.

NOTE: *Active and passive voices are given / receive a thorough introduction in the Verbs chapter of* The Deluxe Transitive Vampire.

not:
The hypotenuse was bored with facing the same old right angle, and its nights were passed in dreams of escape.

but:
The hypotenuse was bored with facing the same old right angle and passed its nights in dreams of escape.

not:
The faun was in love with a nymph named Effie, and many hours were spent each day slinking past her glade.

but:
The faun was in love with a nymph named Effie and spent many hours each day slinking past her glade.

not:
Couples whirled and clomped, tittered and roared till almost dawn, and faux pas were committed on every square foot (and trampled toe) of the ballroom floor.

but:
Couples whirled and clomped, tittered and roared till almost dawn, and committed faux pas on every square foot (and trampled toe) of the ballroom floor.

not:
Dungeons, donjons, and treacherous tollbooths were passed all the way to Trajikistan as we trudged across the continent.

but:
We passed dungeons, donjons, and treacherous tollbooths all the way to Trajikistan as we trudged across the continent.

or:
Trudging across the continent, we passed dungeons, donjons, and treacherous tollbooths all the way to Trajikistan.

↯ The indicative mood is what most sentences take: it states, in one way or another, and also asks questions. The imperative mood is used in issuing commands: You keep your trap shut and your trick cards on the table. If you want an explanation of the subjunctive, go read another book! Had I wished to rephrase that command without the imperative, I could have said: If you want an explanation of the subjunctive, you must go read another book. But this is how the subjunctive mood looks in action:

If those rats were truly vicious, they'd have savaged half these sentences long ago.

The vet insisted that the cat remain under his watchful, professional eye and his certified caresses.

It is advisable that its paw be cradled in cotton and Tiger Balm until the festering has passed its fourth phase.

NOTE: *The faux pas cat is in so much pain, it is no longer a symbol.*

She insisted that he keep her company through the midnight watch and then the Apocalypse.

shifting:
Slip the noose around your neck coquettishly and then you
must ask him wistfully to help you bury the hatchet.

consistent, with indicative mood:
You must slip the noose around your neck coquettishly and
then you must ask him beseechingly to help you bury the
hatchet.

consistent, with imperative mood:
Slip the noose around your neck coquettishly and then ask him
wistfully to help you bury the hatchet.

shifting:
It is essential that this cello remain with our inquisitors and
undergoes a thorough interrogation.

consistent, with subjunctive mood:
It is essential that this cello remain with our inquisitors and
undergo a thorough interrogation.

shifting:
Flee while there is still time and
you should leave your regrets folded
in your possessions.

consistent, with imperative mood:
Flee while there is still time and
leave your regrets folded in your
possessions.

shifting:
Put one magic stone in each cup of your bra and then you should hearken to your wishes.

consistent,
with imperative mood:

Put one magic stone
in each cup of your
bra and then hearken
to your wishes.

consistent, with indicative mood:
You should put one magic stone in each cup of your bra and then you should hearken to your wishes.

vis-à-vis

✦ This isn't really a Francophone's or pompous ass's synonym for *about* or *concerning* in the course of a normal exchange. Where the expression does belong is in proposing or seeking comparisons, stating or asking how one thing is seen in relation to another.

"What's your take on the pandemonium at the Schloss vis-à-vis the commotion in Amplochacha?" asked the nanny of the bandit gagged and bound in the baby dragons' playroom, while the au pair tickled him with a feather from Duchess Ilona's recent molting.

visitant / visitor

❧ A *visitant* is a supernatural being, a phantom; a migratory bird spending a limited time in a particular clime; or, in human form, a pilgrim, a religious sightseer. *Visitant* is rarely used as an ordinary guest or *visitor,* paying a usual social visit.

It was in a clearing not unlike this one that I first encountered the nefarious visitant with wings sprouting out of his hoofs.

The lone visitor at Amplochacha's historical museum that afternoon hovered around a case of Azurikoan ephemera from the reign of Incognito VIII.

where

❧ As Platgut puts it, *at* is already contained in the adverb *where,* when needed, which therefore has no wish to be seen with it.

not:
Where were you born at—or did you just get snorted fully formed out of a tiger angel's nostrils?

but:

Where were you born—or were you simply snorted fully formed out of a tiger angel's nostrils?

"Now where *did* I leave my gloves?" she asked after an unsuccessful rummage in her reticule.

For a cartographer, Jonquil showed a curious confusion about where she'd been when interrogated by the spy ring in Blegue.

which / what

❧ As interrogative adjectives to ask questions about a choice or selection, these two are not interchangeable. *Which* implies choice from a limited number of things, while *what* is the word when the choice is unlimited.

Which pair of fidgety shoes is missing from the cluttered closet of Duchess Ilona?

Where were you born—or were you simply snorted
fully formed out of a tiger angel's nostrils?

What paper do you read for such an odd slant on the vicissitudes of Trajikistani politics?

Which interloper do you suspect
—Frotteau Dessange,
Serafina Dos Equis, or
Drasko Mustafović?

who / whom

⸙ Since two gargoyles are facing off over this subjective/objective puzzle in *The Deluxe Transitive Vampire,* I will posit a mere postscript to these two trouble-causers here (the words, not the gargoyles).

"Who is this for?" asked Jonquil when Torquil handed her a bouquet of tormented tuberoses half-dead from the *Liebestod* Torquil had played at maximum volume all the way from his house to hers (although he was thinking of it at the time as from his hearse to hers). "Who are those from?" he replied, indicating a folly of columbines and peonies frolicking on her harpsichord.

🙥 In everyday exchanges, *who* often appears where *whom* is, strictly speaking, correct. Especially when it's the first word of a statement or question, it sounds more natural: it's the word we expect to find there, which is why we often hear—or say—"Who am I speaking to?" Flaunting immaculate usage, one would say, "To whom am I speaking?" The arch-propriety of using *whom* would be contagious through the rest of the sentence and impel one to avoid ending it with a preposition to boot.*

* I couldn't resist that clumsy conclusion to such an imperious pair of sentences.

who else

🙥 When *who* is accompanied by *else* (which vastly increases the possibilities of this mystery *who*), the possessive is usually *who else's,* not *whose else.*

Who else's favors are you seeking besides the Countess of Troo's?

who's / whose

𝄢 *Who's* can be said to be possessive only when it's the contraction for *who has*. It never means *of whom* or the possessive form of *who*. Most often *who's* is a contraction for *who is*. *Whose* is how *who* possesses.

"Who's got my underarm razor?" skirled the lamia, pretending that she was hirsute in erogenous and other zones.

"Who's that vamp of serpentine grace?" asked one of the judges, nudging as much of the panel as his elbows could vibrate with one swift jab on either side.

Whose black pumps are those walking with a veil down the aisle?

NOTE: *Platgut points out the casual, colloquial language employed by the lamia in that first sentence ("who's got"instead of "who has")—but of course, she's just trying to be one of the girls, in every possible way.*

yours / your's

𝄢 There is no such word as *your's*. It is so nonexistent I shouldn't have included it as part of this entry. It's like saying *who's* as a possessive, the one we just left. It's *yours truly.* Truly, it is. *Yours* is the form for either singular or plural *you.* Startling Glower's "Up Yours" program featured a ballet with errant and superfluous apostrophes meeting grisly deaths at the mercy of enormous white swans (see those long-necked cream puffs in *parallel constructions*) before they could mate with black swans (in the wings) and produce flying mutant marks of punctuation *and* further havoc in this bestial tetralogy of the writer's labyrinth and the languages of Azuriko, Blegue, and Trajikistan.

The ace up my sleeve is mine, not yours, so I shall decide when to play it.

This heart of mine is yours as well, even when it's breaking.

Appendix

Perilous Phrases

LIKE GUESTS AT THE SCHLOSS, phrases are promiscuous, but they can be much more reckless than those rowdy revelers. They'll attach themselves to anyone or anything, they'll do it in the road. Although they don't bring wrack and ruin, they can wreak havoc in your meaning, your intention within a sentence.

We have already seen how dangling and misplaced modifiers often create surrealistic ready-mades, bringing bizarre images to mind, and they do so with great flamboyance when they come in the guise of phrases. The different types of phrases, explored intimately and lingeringly in *The Deluxe Transitive Vampire,* are only here to have fun, not to be re-explained and re-introduced. You may dally with them in both the Verbals and Phrases chapters there should you care to refresh your memory and slake the vampire's thirst.

As I told you earlier, I have gleaned much of my understanding from the final efforts of the departed Natty Ampersand, and many questions were left hanging along with that half a personage. Ampersand makes it clear in his notes, which resemble Beethoven's original scores, that participial phrases are the most dangerous femmes fatales, nymphomaniacs, and priapic cruisers of all. Natty crossed out *grande horizontale* (just as Beethoven crossed out many a note), probably because the metaphor refused to dangle. It is on this basis, anyway, that we are devoting more pages to participial phrases than to the other ones.

Cram Fossilblast also has something to say here—at last! I have cited him less frequently than I had intended to because shortly after making his acquaintance, I made him my love slave and decided to keep him to myself. Well, wasn't he just asking for it, calling himself the Whore of Babel and flashing his irresistible charms?

Before I fell for him and abducted him from the writer's labyrinth, Fossilblast offered the hypothesis that participial phrases cause so much trouble because we rarely use them in speech, especially to begin a sentence: they aren't part of our everyday conversational structures. Infinitive phrases open spoken sentences more often than participial and gerund phrases, but their use in this way is hardly rampant. After Fossilblast imparted this insight, Startling Glower, on "Up Your Eponym," had guests conversing in such an artificial fashion to celebrate Fossilblast's decision not to publish a volume on this issue.

Among *painful separations,* we saw several ill-considered juxtapositions: phrases modifying the wrong noun by being out of place. In some cases the solution is not merely to move the phrase or noun, but to create a new construction with some of grammar's (and your) other forms and tricks, such as replacing the phrase with a clause, its subject clearly the star. Besides verbal phrases, prepositional phrases slither around and show up where they shouldn't belong, except in a reconstructed tableau.

prepositional phrases

misplaced:
With fangs like those, the banal bonbon must meet with the
little vampire's disdain.

  ❧ As it reads above, the bonbon has fangs. Vampires do
  turn their midnight snacks into converts, but we don't
  know that he has bitten this one yet.

rearranged:
With fangs like those, the little vampire must disdain the banal
bonbon.

misplaced:
Among the crème de la crème, the gala was attended by a cow
with a crumpled horn, a pack of obstreperous fantoccini, and a
diamond-studded dummy in furs.

rewritten:
Among the crème de la crème attending the gala were a cow
with a crumpled horn, a pack of obstreperous fantoccini, and a
diamond-studded dummy in furs.

misplaced:
As a paragon of finesse and fashion, I think you should
suppress those boxer shorts and see to those rebel tufts in
your wings.

  ❧ The phrase "as a paragon of finesse and fashion" sets up
  the expectation that the subject immediately following it is

"you"—the one who has a reputation to uphold, and not "I," a mere meddler telling others how to maintain face.

rearranged:
As a paragon of finesse and fashion, you should suppress those boxer shorts and see to those rebel tufts in your wings.

or:
I think that as a paragon of finesse and fashion, you should suppress those boxer shorts and see to those rebel tufts in your wings.

misplaced:
As one of the most glorious structures ever to span a river, Ziggie told us the Cruelty Star North Bridge had withstood the tempest of 1895, the cavalry stampede of 1903, and the rout of the mastodons in 1947.

NOTE: *It is doubtful that Ziggie has such long legs, however glorious her body, and besides, she's talking about the bridge.*

rewritten:
Ziggie told us that the Cruelty Star North Bridge, one of the most glorious structures ever to span a river, had withstood the tempest of 1895, the cavalry stampede of 1903, and the rout of the mastodons in 1947.

"As one of the most glorious structures ever to span a river," said Ziggie, "the Cruelty Star North Bridge withstood the tempest of 1895, the cavalry stampede of 1903, and the rout of the mastodons in 1947."

infinitive phrases

dangling:
To be ultimately satisfying, you should arrange a tryst to coincide with several other transgressions as well.

right:
To be ultimately satisfying, a tryst should be arranged to coincide with several other transgressions as well.

right:
To be ultimately satisfying, a tryst should coincide with several other transgressions as well.

NOTE: *It is quite plausible that the first, dangling example could be intended, if the emphasis is on one of the trysters (giving satisfaction) instead of the meeting itself. But "gratifying" would be a more apt word choice if that is what you have in mind, and two gratifying and gratified trysters, trysting the night away, would create a satisfying tryst.*

dangling:
To keep your life uncomplicated, that Liebfraumilcher is to be avoided, and her mother shunned with all due haste.

rearranged:
To keep your life uncomplicated, you should avoid that
Liebfraumilcher and shun her mother with all due haste.

dangling:
To reach the remoter regions of Trajikistan, serpents in heat
and dragons in distress waylay the wanderluster with lascivious
suggestions and beseeching laments and significantly delay his
progress.

rewritten:
To reach the remoter regions of Trajikistan, the wanderluster
is waylaid by serpents in heat with lascivious suggestions and
dragons in distress with beseeching laments, and finds his
progress significantly delayed.

NOTE: *This sentence would read better if the infinitive phrase construction were dropped altogether or if the sentence began: "In order to reach . . ."*

En route to the remoter regions of Trajikistan, the
wanderluster is waylaid by serpents in heat with lascivious
suggestions, and dragons in distress with beseeching laments,
and finds his progress significantly delayed.

dangling:
To retrieve the robbed reticule, the trouble she took was of no
avail without her missing passport.

reconstructed:
To retrieve the robbed reticule, she found the trouble she took
to be of no avail without her missing passport.

dangling:
To sink his fangs into this gorgeous nanny, every wile and seductive artifice was called upon by the little vampire so that she would bend over him that night just close enough while tucking him into bed.

> ☘ Here, as we will see with Sir Tazzlemunk and the torched angel in *participial phrases,* the passive voice introduces the problem by shifting attention away from the subject belonging to the infinitive phrase—in this case, "the little vampire."

rewritten:
To sink his fangs into this gorgeous nanny, the little vampire called upon every wile and seductive artifice so that she would bend over him that night just close enough while tucking him into bed.

dangling:
To arrive at the Schloss by water, the train you take will leave you at the lake, where Mustafović's boatman will meet you and convey you to the distant shore that shimmers with the light of your desires.

rearranged:
To arrive at the Schloss by water, you take a train to the lake, where you'll be met by Mustafović's boatman and be conveyed to the distant shore that shimmers with the light of your desires.

participial phrases

dangling:
Opening the book, bats flew into our faces.

rewritten, with absolute phrase:
The book opening, bats flew into our faces.

rewritten with dependent clause:
As we opened the book, bats flew into our faces.

dangling:
Rearranging her coiffure, the night opened up before her with
an ominous pause and quiet.

rearranged:
Rearranging her coiffure, she sensed the night opening up
before her with an ominous pause and quiet.

NOTE: *She, not the night, has a coiffure to arrange, and the hands
to do it. Although it is not inconceivable that the night did rearrange
her coiffure, that is not what Strophe Dulac meant in* The Stupor of
Flanelle Lune.

As she arranged her coiffure, the night opened up before her
with an ominous pause and quiet.

dangling:
Deliriously savoring each note, the dragon's mysterious
fragrance went quite to Alyosha's head.

reattached:
Deliriously savoring each note, Alyosha quite lost her head to
the dragon's mysterious fragrance.

dangling:
Undoing the most prepossessing parcel, the yellow and black
ribbon snaked over Lucita's arm.

reribboned:
As Lucita undid the most prepossessing parcel, the yellow and
black ribbon snaked over her arm.

passive voice creating placement havoc when a participial
phrase is present:
Trotting into the piano room, the harping angel was torched
by Sir Tazzlemunk.

   ❦ Remark: The angel couldn't have been trotting in, as the
harp was not a lyre.

rewritten:
Trotting into the piano room, Sir Tazzlemunk torched the
harping angel.

misplaced:
Torso trundled a cart of pastries to the duchess, the au pair,
and the duenna smothered in frosting and crème fraîche.

rearranged:
Torso trundled a cart of pastries smothered in frosting and crème fraîche to the duchess, the au pair, and the duenna. (The baby dragons were cavorting under the table and snapping at his trouser legs.)

misplaced:
Navigating her way through the boutique, bras and panties cried out to her hands to thrill to them.

Tottering uneasily on high heels, slips and nighties called to her to touch them.

presented more plausibly:
As she navigated her way through the boutique, bras and panties cried out to her hands to thrill to them.

Tottering uneasily on high heels, she heard slips and nighties calling to her to touch them.

> ❧ Remark: The example above has brought a new participial phrase into this froufrou bazaar—but also in its rightful place.

an ambiguous example of a misplaced participial phrase:
He was the only rat in the gang wearing sunglasses.

> ❧ The placement of "wearing sunglasses" creates ambiguity. Is this a motley assortment of animals all wearing sunglasses and toting guns, with our fellow the only rat amongst them? Or is this a gang of rats—or anything else—

none of whom is wearing sunglasses except the rat to whom that pronoun "he" refers?

Of all the rat gang members, only he was wearing sunglasses.

He was the only rat wearing
sunglasses in the gang.

dangling:
Scampering away together into a torrid jungle of emotions, an equivocal elation could be felt.

re-placed:
Scampering away together into a torrid jungle of emotions, they could feel an equivocal elation.

Scampering away together into a torrid jungle of emotions, they were equivocally elated.

dangling:
Dismantling all ethics and appearances, a soothing destiny could be slithered into and be given no more thought.

fixed:
Dismantling all ethics and appearances, she could slither into a soothing destiny without giving it any more thought.

dangling:
Looking down to the west, there's an immense coral reef where the mermaids gather to scratch their backs and rough up their riffs and amplify their repertoire.

rearranged:
Looking to the west, you'll see an immense coral reef where the mermaids gather to scratch their backs and rough up their riffs and amplify their repertoire.

or:

To the west rests an immense coral reef where the mermaids gather to scratch their backs and rough up their riffs and amplify their repertoire.

NOTE: *Cram Fossilblast points out a band of renegades that have turned into prepositions: participles that can kick off a phrase at the start of a sentence without running the usual risks, so that they need not* *refer to the subject of the sentence. These privileged mongrels include* concerning, considering, regarding, assuming, barring, following, given, granted, provided.

Considering how far we have traveled since daybreak, it might be sheer folly to scale that cliff without a loll and a snack beneath those blighted elms.

Provided that Drasko Mustafović falls for the scheme, there's a good chance the roof of the Schloss will double as a terrace café and widow's walk for the wives of his band of brigands.

Assuming the slate and other materials arrive in time, work could begin as soon as next month, with a troupe of strapping, handsome craftsmen crawling through the windows and over the roof all hours of day and night.

Given that the baby dragons can't climb the stairs with skateboards strapped to their bellies, we should be able to carry on and caterwaul without interruption and their voracious importunities.

gerund phrases

dangling:
Before pasting his photograph into her bestiary, a telegram was handed to her.

right:
Before pasting his photograph into her bestiary, she was handed a telegram about a dangerous liaison.

right:
Before pasting his photograph into her bestiary, she received a telegram coupling trouble with fun.

> ⸙ Remark: It's not the telegram that's pasting his photo into her collection of beasts and brutes, and that is the misimpression the first sentence conveys.

dangling:
While dreaming of baboons and palindromes, her slumbers were interrupted by a hand poised on her throat.

right:
While dreaming of baboons and palindromes, she was interrupted from her slumbers by a hand poised on her throat.

> ⸙ Her slumbers were not dreaming: they were merely providing the slowed-down brain waves conducive to dreams. *She* was dreaming, so "she" should follow the descriptive phrase.

dangling:
While pushing the pram along the avenida in shirtsleeves, a
great apprehension came over me.

⸎ Restoring the pram-pushing to a human agent:

While pushing the pram along the avenida in shirtsleeves, I
was overcome by a great apprehension.

⸎ Ludicrous extremes await us as we try to get the shirt off
the avenida:

While pushing the pram in shirtsleeves . . .
In shirtsleeves, I while pushing the pram . . .
Overcome by a great apprehension in shirtsleeves . . .

Sentence Creation and Elaboration

EMPHASIS, UNITY, AND COHERENCE make a sentence come across, its meaning evident or provoking one to find it. Although short sentences can deliver a wallop when used sparingly, in the right instances, they give a choppy, monotonous, or cretinous impression if used in rapid succession, too often, or carelessly. Short, blasted sentences can be combined in many ways, creating or revealing relationships, reveling in more exciting rhythms. Rhythm is as important to a well-written sentence as is grammatical savvy. In the following cascade of variations, short simple sentences show off these transformations before winding up at the Schloss, where everyone awaits you.

The travelers rubbed their eyes. They were weary. They couldn't believe them. It was so trite. It was a mirage. The mirage was made of clouds, a stream of gold, some fabulous animals, and some old shoes.

Unable to believe their eyes, the weary travelers rubbed them, for the mirage, made of clouds, a stream of gold, some fabulous animals, and some old shoes, was so trite.

The weary travelers rubbed their disbelieving eyes at the sight of the trite mirage, which was made of clouds, a stream of gold, some fabulous animals, and old shoes.

He was sadistic. His particular specialty was contumely. Miranda craved it. She was thirsty for it. This thirst was abject.

Abjectly thirsting, Miranda craved his particular sadistic specialty, which was contumely.

Contumely, his particular sadistic specialty, is what Miranda craved with an abject thirst.

His particular sadistic specialty was contumely, which Miranda craved with an abject thirst.

Yolanta became inebriated. She felt a rage for life. It was surging. A truculent new trauma caused this. She was yanked out of her stupor.

Yanked out of her stupor by a truculent new trauma, Yolanta became inebriated with a surging rage for life.

A truculent new trauma yanking her out of her stupor, Yolanta became inebriated with a surging rage for life.

Surging with a rage for life, Yolanta was yanked out of her stupor by a truculent new trauma.

He had made her acquaintance. It was amiable. She was a purveyor of ambrosias. She was lying asprawl. She was on a divan. She was in pajamas. The divan was of a curious Persian design.

He had made the amiable acquaintance of a pajama'd purveyor of ambrosias who was lying asprawl a divan of a curious Persian design.

Lying asprawl a curiously Persian divan was the ambrosia purveyor he'd met in pajamas.

NOTE: *We've just hit a placement conundrum. Was he or she wearing pajamas? Maybe they both were. But if you want Ms. Ambrosia in pajamas, you'd find her like this:*

Lying asprawl a curious Persian divan was the ambrosia purveyor in pajamas whose acquaintance he'd amiably made.

NOTE: *In the above version, she was wearing pajamas on the occasion of this sentence, not necessarily when they'd previously met.*

Lying asprawl a Persian divan and wearing pajamas was the ambrosia purveyor whose amiable acquaintance he'd made.

In pajamas and lying asprawl a Persian divan was the ambrosia purveyor whose amiable acquaintance he'd made.

The ravine gaped. The heat was stupendous. The bandits pursued their course. It was insidious and cupidinous.

In the stupendous heat, the bandits pursued their insidious, cupidinous course through the gaping ravine.

Although the heat was stupendous and the ravine gaping, the bandits pursued their insidious, cupidinous course.

Insidiously pursuing their cupidinous course through the staggering heat, the bandits traversed the yawning ravine.

Through the staggeringly hot and yawning ravine, the bandits pursued their insidious, cupidinous course.

The bandits, pursuing their insidious, cupidinous course through the stupendous heat, were swallowed by the gaping ravine.

Her garret was rickety. It was crawling with rats. Jonquil sat at her computer. This went on for hours. She was concocting implausible itineraries. They were on marvelous made-up maps.

Sitting at her computer in her rickety garret crawling with rats, Jonquil spent hours concocting implausible itineraries on marvelous made-up maps.

In her rickety garret, which was crawling with rats, Jonquil sat at her computer for hours concocting implausible itineraries on made-up maps.

The impostor gloated. The last piece of his little triumph was in place. It had fallen there deftly. His eyes glimmered craftily.

His eyes glimmering craftily, the impostor gloated over the last piece of his little triumph as it fell deftly into place.

The last piece of his little triumph having fallen deftly into place, the impostor gloated with craftily glimmering eyes.

The megalomaniac was scudding. He crossed the vestibule. His harem was waiting for him. They were in an uproar. They were all jabbering at once. Their jewels flashed like eyes. Their eyes flashed like knives.

His harem awaiting him in an uproar, their jewels flashing like eyes, their eyes like knives, the megalomaniac came scudding across the vestibule as they jabbered all at once.

Jabbering all at once and flashing their eyes like knives, their jewels like eyes, the uproarious harem greeted the megalomaniac scudding across the vestibule.

Scudding across the vestibule into a jabbering harem of eye-flashing jewels and knife-flashing eyes, the megalomaniac was home!

The megalomaniac came scudding across the vestibule into his impatient uproar of a harem with their eyes like knives and jewels like eyes.

Across the vestibule and into the jabbering, flashing uproar of his harem scuttled the megalomaniac.

The train clacked along. The conductor was thumbing a girlie magazine. He was singing "Makin' Whoopee." He was cockeyed.

As the train clacked along, the cockeyed conductor thumbed a girlie magazine and sang "Makin' Whoopee."

Thumbing a girlie magazine and singing "Makin' Whoopee," the cockeyed conductor clacked along in the train.

Cockeyed, the conductor thumbed a girlie magazine and sang "Makin' Whoopee" in the clacking-along train.

One thumb in a girlie magazine and "Makin' Whoopee" on his lips, the cockeyed conductor pleasantly distracted himself as the train clacked along.

They left Incognito V's body. It was lying in state. It lay there for three days. At this time from all over the kingdom his subjects rode bicycles. They rode them into the city. They went to pay their respects. They did this on two wheels. The monarch had wished this. He said so as he was dying. He loved Flann O'Brien very much.

They left Incognito V's body lying in state for three days, while from all over the kingdom his subjects rode bicycles into the city to pay their respects on two wheels, for that was the monarch's dying wish (he loved Flann O'Brien very much).

During the three days that Incognito V's body lay in state, from all over the kingdom his subjects rode bicycles into the city to pay their respects. A great lover of Flann O'Brien, the monarch had expressed this wish as he lay dying.

Lying in state for three days, Incognito V's body received last respects from bicyclists all over the kingdom, in accordance with the dying wishes of the monarch, a great lover of Flann O'Brien.

The Grand Rewrite and One Final, Lasting Invitation to the Reader

PEOPLE CAME TO THE SCHLOSS. They were visitors. Usually they were welcome. That's when they brought prosciutto* and truffles in hampers. They demurely responded when someone spoke to them. They kept their feet off the divans. Other times they were clumsy. They came marauding. They trampled the dahlias and foxglove. They tampered with their hostess. They tore apart their beds and filled them with their many bodies. Crumbs were left behind by them. Curlers were to be found too in their beds.

* prosciutto: Spell-check says this should read *prostitute,* but that is not what I meant. Not even the Whore of Babel was tucked into a picnic basket.

Ameliorated:
The Schloss's visitors were not always welcome intruders who bore hampers groaning with prosciutto and truffles, and who acquiesced when spoken to and kept their feet off the divans—but were sometimes inept marauders who trampled the dahlias and foxglove and tampered with their hostess and left crumbs and curlers among their tousled and crowded beds.

Modus operandi:
Short choppy sentences were combined through participial phrases and subordinate clauses. Passive voice changed to active at end. Simple sentences were turned into descriptive passages. Action/behavior turned into name-calling.

Index

About the Author

KAREN ELIZABETH GORDON is the author of *The Deluxe Transitive Vampire, The New Well-Tempered Sentence, The Disheveled Dictionary, The Ravenous Muse, The Red Shoes and Other Tattered Tales,* and *Paris Out of Hand: A Wayward Guide.* She divides her time between Berkeley, California, and France.